Ready, Set . . . Wait

May God strengthen you
in every way.

Karen Barber

Ready, Set . . . Wait

Help for Life on Hold

Karen Barber

Baker Books

A Division of Baker Book House Co
Grand Rapids, Michigan 49516

Published by Baker Books
a division of Baker Book House Company
P.O. Box 6287, Grand Rapids, MI 49516-6287

Printed in the United States of America

Library of Congress Cataloging-in-Publication Data

Barber, Karen, 1953–
    Ready, set . . . wait : help for life on hold / Karen Barber.
      p. cm.
    ISBN 0-8010-5712-4 (pbk.)
    1. Christian life. 2. Conduct of life. I. Title.
BV4501.2.B3827 1996
248.4—dc20   95-10264

Scripture not otherwise identified is taken from the HOLY BIBLE, NEW INTERNATIONAL VERSION®. NIV®. Copyright © 1973, 1978, 1984 by International Bible Society. Used by permission of Zondervan Publishing House. All rights reserved. Other versions used are Good News Bible (GNB) and King James Version (KJV).

Words to the song "I Am" are copyright by Tricia Steedley Cudd and used with permission.

To those who have
allowed me to share their stories
within these pages:
Thank you
for opening up your hearts and lives
to the glory of God.

Contents

Wait Broke the Wagon

I ignored the first dinner call echoing down the basement stairway and slouched farther down into the cranky springs of the vintage red velvet chair with the flat arms as wide as ironing boards. Back in the sixties it was my TV throne, the place where I escaped the summer heat and let my mind be lulled by the netherworld of black-and-white game shows.

My stomach growled. Admittedly, I was a bit hungry, but if I just lingered a few more moments, the napkins and forks would already be placed around the walnut table upstairs and I would get to see which of the three bachelorettes was about to be chosen on *The Dating Game*.

"Karen!" my father's voice rattled again from upstairs.

"Wait!" I cried. "The show's almost over."

And then came the reply so redolent of my dad's midwestern upbringing that you could almost smell the newly-mown hay fields. "Wait?" Dad cajoled, "why, wait broke the wagon!"

Even at twelve, I recognized blank-faced, irrefutable truth. No rational argument gurgled into my throat. Indeed, there was nothing to do except obey. I got up and snapped off the TV.

Now that I am grown, Dad's old-fashioned witticism that played on the homonyms *weight* and *wait* still sticks clearly in my mind. Since those preteen days, I have learned that at times the utter mental and emotional weight of awaiting things in my life has indeed overloaded me to the point of breaking down body, mind, and spirit. In others words, wait has broken my wagon.

We do not have to convince anyone that waiting is the black eye of life. Waiting has plagued humanity since ancient times. Technology may have streamlined, computerized, and microwaved us, but waiting has not become obsolete like spoked, wooden wagon wheels with handwrought iron rims.

Waiting can be divided into two categories: the ordinary wait and something much bigger that I term "the Wait." The ordinary wait consists of those unwelcome and bothersome intervals during the course of our days: dead time in lines, in doctors' offices, and at traffic lights. The ordinary wait is irritating but can be managed and endured decently if we fill it up with some portable, productive activity like eating an apple, chatting, listening to our Walkman, or furiously jotting notes in our pocket planner.

The Wait, however, is not so easily tamed. Take the ordinary wait and multiply it by mammoth time: weeks, months, years, decades. Then up the ante a thousand times on the reward we are awaiting. Tie the reward to our deepest emotional desires and lifelong dreams, things that well from the very core of our being and for which no other substitute will ever really ever do. These lifelong dreams usually do not go away over time nor fade with repeated disappointment. In fact, disappointments sometimes intensify these yearnings to unmanageable proportions. We have been trying with all of our hearts, minds, and souls to attain our dreams. Unfortunately, we are still waiting.

The longed-for events generally fall into the categories of recovery, reconciliation, and achievement tied to affirmation. These lifelong dreams and hopes are long-term quests that are quite specific to each individual during different ages of life.

For some, the Wait is toward recovery. It means surviving a catastrophe and struggling toward the day when life will again be stable and productive. The causes of the struggles are themselves quite diverse: divorce, bankruptcy, bereavement, failure, accident, disability, disaster, unemployment, and physical or mental illness.

For others, the Wait is for a future time of reconciliation or connection into meaningful relationships with others. It might mean weathering the waywardness of a child, a spouse, or a dear one as we await their reconciliation to us, to another person, or even to God. Some of us long to find that special someone who will bring new joy and meaning into our lives. For a single person, the Wait is the lonesome time searching for a life partner; for the infertile couple, the Wait is the roller coaster years of longing for a child.

Finally, the Wait may be for achievement. The specific goal can be mastery in nearly any field: becoming first vice president, having a winning football record, getting published, affording a dream house, becoming district superintendent, receiving a college degree, being named volunteer of the year, owning one's own business, making a contribution to knowledge. Although the goals may be dissimilar, the affirmation they represent is not. All achievements have in common the quest for final, complete affirmation of our worth. In our quests for accomplishment, we seek the elusive life event that will at last bestow upon us personal or public respect and acclaim.

Whether we await recovery, reconciliation, or achievement, this is the Wait. I define the Wait as the time we already have spent, plus the unknown quantity of time we may yet spend, awaiting a significant, positive goal or change in our lives. Not only is there no specific nor predictable due date for these goals and changes, but there is absolutely no present assurance of their eventual attainment.

An example will help us distinguish the difference between the ordinary wait and the Wait. A pregnant woman awaiting the birth of a child is not experiencing the Wait. Although it might cover a long anxious period of time, she has the advantage of predictable closure which we, by definition, do not have in the Wait. The woman not only has a due date, but the examining doctor can make sure the baby is developing properly by measuring benchmarks of normal growth at any given time along the way. Admittedly, there may be complications and delays in the pregnancy. It could be a boy instead of a girl, and there is the slight chance that she will lose the baby. But in approximately nine months, the woman's time will definitely come, for better or for worse.

On the other hand, an infertile woman awaiting conception is involved in no ordinary wait; she is under the heavy burden of none other than the Wait. Her maternal desires may be just as strong as her already pregnant friend's, but she has no formulas which spew out an assured future. Will she conceive next month, this year, or ever?

For her there are no sure benchmarks that might measure progress. Conception has either taken place this month or it has not, and there absolutely is no way to guess how close she has come. Therefore, the woman is torn between whether to pursue and prepare or whether to totally abandon the whole idea and go another direction with the precious days of her life. If she busies herself with baby magazines, crib shopping, and layette planning, she could be setting herself up for horrible heartache each time she steps into the empty nursery.

Although our longings may be diverse—for a child, a promotion, a healing, a reconciliation, an affirmation—we all are comrades in the Wait. We share common feelings, needs, and tribulations. We live with uncertainty, brokenness, soul searching, and daily, hourly endurance. Accordingly, we can learn much from each other.

How can such a problematic life be successfully lived? Together in these pages we will acknowledge our pain, experience, and continuing anguish. This book is our beginning point, an illustration of what life is teaching us. We will seek biblical sense and common sense. We will snatch wisdom from our failures. What we set about to do here will be completed only by our own unique living testimonies of faithful endurance.

Beyond the Fairness Rules

One gray morning I was jogging around a deserted road in our rural subdivision. Suddenly a low growl caused me to stumble in fright. A dog as black as soot had been lying on the roadside just in front of me and had been startled into white-eyed terror by my approach. My fear turned to anger as I realized someone had dumped the poor creature there on the roadside!

I jogged home and stuffed two stale hamburger buns into my pockets, hoping the dog would have traveled on when I returned. He had not. Instead he had arranged himself in a bony hump in the same graceless, dusty spot right there on top of the curb next to a broken beer bottle. "He's no one's dog," I thought. And so he was named.

When No One's Dog saw me, he was spooked again. He galloped to the edge of the woods and threw back his head in a fast schizophrenic yelp. I tensed, inched forward to "his" spot, deposited the bread, backed away, and then walked briskly up the road. Finally, I looked over my shoulder, satisfied with the glimpse of No One's Dog scuttling over to inhale the splintery bread.

It became painfully apparent that No One's Dog was waiting. Days went by, but he kept faithfully to that spot. That was where his owner had left him, and that was the magical place where he would again be found. Never mind that there was no food nor shelter. Never mind that if it rained, the dusty spot turned into an orange mud hole.

If anyone should have been loved and rewarded for his long-suffering fidelity, it was No One's Dog. He was not. We all understand that his owner never returned. That is what makes the saga of No One's Dog so disturbing. It hits the inner buttons marked injustice, indignation, anger, helplessness, and a thousand other feelings we dare not put into words.

The dog's lot was devastating, inexcusable, and spirit crushing, but the unvarnished truth is that we, too, are waiting without guarantees, perhaps even waiting completely in vain. Once we face this fact, we can see the absolute futility of treating our life quests like an ordinary wait. The dog's gigantic mistake was to apply the orderly principles he had learned from the ordinary wait to this extraordinary Wait. In the past, if he just bided his time, his master had always eventually returned.

Our wagons are bound to break down irreparably when we treat gigantic life quests like the post office line where fairness rules apply. At the post office we know for sure that sometime, before we crawl under the bed sheets tonight, we eventually will make it to the postal window. Sometime. Very soon. Right after the lady in the red coat.

Unfortunately, in the Wait our turn at life's window may not come today. Nor tomorrow. In fact, it may never come, even though we have been waiting a very long time, much longer than others already served. We cannot estimate durations by how fast the line is moving; we cannot rank order by arrival time; we cannot expect that line crashers will be censored. No amount of fill-in activities, timetable planning, preparation, or patience will satisfy such inequities.

The sound principles of time management fall sadly apart in the Wait as well. We cannot easily lay our finger on some inefficiency to remedy our dilemma. Since we have already tried everything we know to do, we must accept the delay as somehow due to circumstances beyond our control and possibly beyond all human control. Remember, No One's Dog was dumped. He had no say in the matter. Someone pushed him out of a car door and sped off. The same thing has happened to all of us.

Such open-ended matters are against everything we have been taught in our culture. It is no surprise that we might attempt to solve the puzzle by deciding that the Wait is not a time problem after all. We might speculate that perhaps No One's Dog was a nuisance dog and brought his problems on himself. Maybe he dug up the petunias or scratched holes in the screen door. Perhaps he did something nasty to bring on this rude fate. This may be quite true but strangely it is of little matter now.

By turning a duration problem into a character problem we do nothing but unnecessarily punish those already victimized by unyielding time. In this book we shall set aside any discussions of whether or not we were in any way at fault for our current lot. We shall deal with this uneasy guilt over the past in the next chapter, but for now the healthy thing to do is to lay it aside. Whatever the cause, we must accept the fact that we now are living in the middle of nowhere, and that is where we are going to have to wait and to grow and to prosper.

No One's Dog was without a single possession save one—hope. It was heart rending and ridiculous. It was unbending and unreasonable. Although he was just a dog, he somehow knew that hope is the only way to keep going during the Wait. Our turn just may come. Someday. Maybe tomorrow. This hope is a good and glorious thing. If no impossible dreams were cherished, no long-term accomplishments would ever become reality, no new horizons would ever be gained.

We find hope an integral part of the dictionary definition of waiting, which says that waiting involves not only the stopping, delaying, or holding steady of the present position but also includes the hope or expectation of a favorable change. Therein lies the power. We will wait on very slim chances, but we wait because of the slim chance, not despite it.

The Wait poses very special problems because of the monstrous amounts of time involved. Hope, optimism, and even a clear picture of our current chances are hard to sustain over long, uncertain periods. We are hot then cold, encouraged one day then shattered to pieces the next. Sometimes we meet disappointment with bravado; at other times we face it like our doom. Always lurking deep inside is this nagging thought: Just give it all up; go for something simpler, easier, more obtainable. Summer and winter, feast and famine, that is the unpredictable climate of the Wait.

No Such Thing as Patience

Now that we have defined our problem, we might anticipate a careful treatise on patience. I looked up *patience* in the dictionary and was rattled to learn that the Latin root word means literally to suffer. No thanks.

I am not going to espouse patience as an answer. There are several reasons. For one, I believe patience is rare. We need look no farther than our own experience of ordinary waits to prove that the term "patient person" is an oxymoron. The truth is, no living soul can ever be completely and sweetly and resignedly patient.

Certainly we have different toleration levels in given situations based on the difficulty of the activity, our personalities, and whatever else is presently pressing on us and consuming our mental, physical, and emotional reserves. But at some point we all hit the wall. Show me a mother being "patient" with a tantrum-throwing two-year-old over the candy bins at the grocery checkout, and I will show you a mother who has just arrived home from a week long Caribbean cruise and is still overjoyed to see the rascally little tyke. Either that, or I will show you a mother so bedraggled that she has given up ever trying to tame the monster and is tuning him completely out. It is even quite possible that the "patient" mother is faking it and will explode later and fan the child's britches in the minivan.

Aside from our present ability to cope, we all have our own personal nemesis that will unglue us quite faithfully and repeatedly with very little provocation. It usually is reminiscent of dreadful past experience of being similarly trapped. My bane happens to be killer lines, the kind that curls out of office doors, down corridors, and around the block the day after the deadline for new car license tags. Killer lines make me feel angry, faceless, ill tempered, second class, physically shaken, and powerless.

Whatever form our Waterloo takes, it evokes in us the same out-of-control feelings. Our pet peeve might be pokey, inconsiderate drivers, or incompetent bumblers like the cashier who drops our credit card down a crack in the counter and has to call maintenance, or a droner who spends thirty minutes telling us just two minutes worth of useful information.

Not only is patience quite rare, but it also is overrated. I recently passed a church sign that read, "Patience is the keenest of virtues." I got to thinking about it, and I beg to differ. Usually we are forced to wait by circumstances beyond our control. If it were up to us, we would be finished with the whole tedious business before it even started. So to "patiently" endure is no real virtue. If we are being tranquil and well behaved and accepting, it really benefits our own blood pressure. If we are mad and aggressive, our own stomachs will pay, others will probably get nasty, and there will be an unpleasant scene. What other true choice do we have but to be civilized and be nicely "patient"?

To pick a biblical example, consider "the patience of Job." I give him opening credit; when he loses his children and possessions he does declare, "The LORD gave, and the LORD hath taken away; blessed be the name of the LORD" (Job 1:21). Unbelievable! But later he finally hit the wall. Listen to this:

> In his great power God becomes like clothing to me; he binds me like the neck of my garment. He throws me into the mud, and I am reduced to dust and ashes. "I cry out to you, O God, but you do not answer; I stand up and you merely look at me . . . The churning inside me never stops; days of suffering confront me" (Job 30:18–20, 27).

Shocking. And yet, deep down inside, we know it intimately. We all have been soothed and even scolded by the words, "Be patient. There's got to be a reason." My view is that telling people to be patient is tantamount to telling them to deny their feelings and to negate the bone-crunching impossibility of their current lot in life. It is the old buck-up, cheer-up, get-with-it, melt-in-the-mouth platitude. And unfortunately, it is completely bankrupt of help and consolation. Being patient is definitely not a Band-Aid we can stick across the Wait to trick ourselves into feeling better in our heads.

So please, as we continue this book, let us be honest about our feelings and so restless that we search, grapple, seek, and question. Patience cannot be manufactured. It is merely a by-product of healthy ways of living.

Pure, determined patience got No One's Dog nowhere. There could have been a happy ending to No One's Dog's plight. A neighbor was willing to adopt him and take him to her home, but the dog did not understand. Tragically, he died along the roadside, a victim of an accident, despite our efforts and those of the animal warden to catch him. The Wait had broken down his wagon, and he had lost his flexibility

to trust in something new or beyond his present understanding. He had spent his time running away from help instead of going toward it.

We all are like No One's Dog. We are involved in compli-
cated situations with too many variables to count. We do not
know when we should change course, whom to trust. There
is no magic wand that grants wishes. But we already have
something else much more powerful: grace. God wants to
help us in very practical ways, to direct us, to feed us, to comfort us, to sustain us.

At first, this too sounds vague and unreachable and,
frankly, too pat and simple. In the balance of this book we
shall see that it is anything but simple to face honestly the
issues of the Wait. In these pages we will break away from
unhealthy patterns of the bondage—hoop jumping as I call
it—trying to live up to impossible ideals of being "good
enough" or "ready" for our dreams. We will lay bare our
hunger for the future—the gnawing that feels so physically
painful we think we are about to die.

Many times we will need to step outside of our culture
to challenge ideas of bottom-line thinking, end products,
and success. Instead we will meet helpful role models who
will point us toward a renewed appreciation of the entire
creative process, allowing us to affirm and enjoy not only
who we hope to be but also who we presently are in God's
sight.

As hard as it is to admit, we will uncover our jealousy toward
others who presently possess the blessings we so fervently desire, and we will find new ways to remain in satisfying relationship with such people. We will renew our lost sense of
humor and then go about the business of making ourselves
feel at home during stays of exile in unlikely situations.

In the face of painful Waits, we will find prayer models to
keep our prayer lives healthy when we are frustrated by long-
term unanswered petitions; we will rediscover ancient se-
crets for outlasting pain. Finally, we will be ready to discover

what our heavenly Father, not Hollywood, has planned for us in the very end.

Welcome to the Wait. Here we are broken-down wagons, every one. Since we all are sidelined together right now, we have plenty of time to meditate, explore, and talk. Exactly what can we learn from each other while we are all stuck quite squarely here in the Wait?

Jumping through Hoops

2

Is for Poodles

*S*everal years ago I eagerly traced the progress of one of my novels all the way up to the acquisitions editors' meeting. Just when I expected to be signing a contract, no one at the publishing house would answer my phone calls. Finally, I was given a curt, impersonal "We're overcommitted in that category, but be assured that we have thoroughly reviewed your work." I didn't even get so much as a dry, consoling crumb about what a decent writer I was.

In this deflated, needy, wounded state that only those who have experienced a major setback in the Wait can possibly understand, I sought solace in a women's prayer group. There I scribbled this request: "Please pray for God's help and direction in having my book published."

After the meeting, a pleasant-faced matron sought me out and said matter-of-factly, "About getting a book published. It won't happen until you give God all the glory."

I stood there in shock. The woman barely knew my name; how did she know if I was doing a terrible or a spectacular job of giving God the glory? Besides, she did not understand that I was a magazine ghost writer; I enabled people to tell stories of faith without so much as my own name appearing anywhere in the publication! The woman rattled on, as if her macabre words were meant to soothe me, "You never know. Some people's works are published posthumously."

We mentioned Job in chapter 1, and in this chapter we mention Job's "comforters." They were the "friends" like Zophar who said such things as, "Come on, now, Job. If you were living right, your sufferings would end and God would bless you" (see Job 11:13–18).

There I stood at the close of the meeting, able only to blink in reply at this ancient Zophar masquerading as a modern matron. I stitched my wiggling mouth shut lest I burst out, "Go ahead and say that again after you've been through four-teen years of rejections, trying to write while you're raising three kids, working every volunteer job at the church, and moving eight times. Do you know how often I've been tempted to give up writing and do something where I could actually see some progress like scrubbing shower mildew and soap scum?"

Being civil and a southern lady, I bit my tongue and said none of these things. I instead simply turned heel and fled from this absurd Mrs. Zophar as fast as my sensible sandals could carry me. I cranked up my van feeling unjustly accused and completely worn out. I was suddenly disgusted with the whole idea of dreams if it meant endlessly having to sur-mount obstacles only to be slapped with one more impos-sible criterion after another. I later recorded my thoughts and feelings in my journal:

> Is this "giving God all the glory" another hoop I have to jump through to get published? I feel deep down inside me the im-possibility of the task, as if it's a point I'll never reach. I feel,

indeed, like someone seeking healing who's told to believe harder, or to pray better, or do whatever else they lack in their spiritual life that would finally make them ready for healing.

The personal lesson I'm learning is *never* to tell people that there's some lesson of faith they must master before they can receive something they long for. I admit, lessons can be learned in waiting, but they also can be learned in receiving. Of course, always, and at all times, I can learn more about giving God the glory, but I'm not going to see it as a hoop to jump through before I can have a book published.

Hoop jumping brings to mind a picture of a trained-poodle circus act. The dog's toenails are polished red, and he is wearing a perky vest with gold braid. For some reason, somebody thought it would seem terribly clever to see the creature jump through a hoop. At first, bounding through a ring was the farthest thing from any poodle's mind, but now the dog obliges, not because he likes such antics but because once he has done it, a rewarding doggie snack will be stuck into his woolly mouth.

Until I met Mrs. Zophar, I had not fully appreciated the bondage that spiritual hoop jumping heaps on people already overloaded by the Wait. Such thinking leads us to believe that our dreams are on hold because we have not yet jumped through the proper hoop; we have not yet developed the proper character traits; we have not yet confessed the right sin. Our emotions rightly reply that this is utter nonsense. The burden of unrealized dreams is heavy enough without compounding it with this unwieldy load of blame. That is why our very first topic of discussion in this book must be about liberating ourselves from misplaced inner guilt concerning this waiting period.

Before we go on, let me affirm that I wholeheartedly believe in gently sharing constructive suggestions and advice with one another. A loving and thoughtful insight, rightly spoken, is not only entirely appropriate but often life changing. However, we need to use extreme caution when trying to explain delayed timing in someone else's life with pious sounding answers about what still is not quite right inside.

Admittedly, Mrs. Zophar was dead right about my shortcomings. That did not necessarily make her correct in assuming that spiritual pride was the overriding reason my book had not yet been picked up by a publisher. Yes, I probably did not know how to adequately give God the honor and glory he deserved, and I still do not. Mrs. Zophar was playing the odds like a Las Vegas pro. She could have just as easily fingered any one of my spiritual, mental, or physical disciplines and still have nailed me. She could have said, "Karen, you know your prayer life isn't what it ought to be," "You throw away the church quarterly and the insurance magazine without reading it" or, "You never fertilize your potted plants." Take your pick. She would have been in all cases and in all degrees, profoundly and eerily accurate about my myriad shortcomings.

What Mrs. Zophar was really doing was making a feeble human attempt at answering what I hold to be one of those presently unanswerable questions of the Wait. If there really were an answer to "Why not yet?" we gladly would pay any price of sacrifice, obedience, penance, self-abasement, or restitution to remedy it right away and finally obtain our long-sought dream. But the only sensible thing to do is honestly to admit that we cannot say exactly why any of us has yet to receive his or her heart's desire.

Unfortunately, this is a truth we seldom understand until we have exhausted ourselves jumping through hoops. We need to free ourselves from this fruitless and constant frenzy, because there are many other infinitely more constructive things to be done during the Wait. Let us examine several of these hoops and apply some good, old-fashioned, biblical sense to them.

The Worthiness Hoop

Mrs. Zophar has already introduced us to the worthiness hoop. Interestingly enough, this feeling of unworthiness does not always need an outside voice to form words around it. I once spoke with a young woman who had been waiting a long time to meet the right marriage partner. After the traumatic breakup of yet another relationship, she related the following experience:

> One day I had like a breakdown. As a teenager, I'd been rebellious, and I kept thinking about all of the bad things I'd done. I figured that was why God was punishing me now. I called a church counselor and started crying and told her about my pain and my unworthiness and how I'd messed up my life so bad that I wouldn't blame God if he never did anything good for me. All of a sudden I realized that the counselor was crying too, and finally she said, "God isn't punishing you. He's grieving with you over your heartbreak and your loneliness." She said that I could get rid of those bad things in the past. That's what the cross was for. We prayed, and then the counselor said, "Tell me what your ideal marriage partner would be like." At first I couldn't even say anything, because it was hard to believe that God loved me and cared about me and that it was even possible to ask him for anything.

Like this young woman, we all sometimes start feeling flawed and defeated during long Waits. The thought hammers away in our heads, "Why are others getting blessed with what I want so badly and I'm not? I must not be doing things right, or maybe I'm being punished for something I've done wrong in the past."

Such feelings about ourselves follow the dog-master picture. The counselor tried to make the desperate young woman understand that if God were a poodle trainer who fed only good doggies, then every one of us would be in mortal trouble. If goodness were the only criterion for blessing, we should all be living on the dark side of the moon with nothing to sustain even the tiniest drop of life. No one would ever get healed or have a baby or get married or become vice president of marketing or make the United States Olympic Team.

It would be interesting to go back to our original list of reasons for the Wait in chapter 1 and take a straw vote about which ones were caused by the individual and which ones were not. For instance, we might easily vote that certain recovery Waits caused by an accident, a natural disaster, the death of a loved one, or a physical illness were, most likely, not the fault of the victim. Interestingly enough, the vote would not be unanimous. These calamities were the very things that befell Job. Even the freak nature of Job's problems did not prevent his friends from vigorously claiming it was all decidedly and completely his fault. Without even the benefit of anesthesia, these friends pulled out their religious scalpels, ready to do major exploratory surgery on poor, squirming Job.

Things become even more muddled when we attempt to take a decisive vote on whether or not we are to blame in other recovery, relationship, and achievement Waits. For instance: divorce, unemployment, wayward children, and unpublished novels. Most of us would be in a true quandary about whether to vote yes or no on the personal blame in such cases. Yes, in some cases we indeed have been partially responsible for our plights. Yes, we have made choices that in retrospect we realize were not the best. But on the other hand there are divorced people who have been faithful spouses, unemployed people who have been model employees, loving parents who must endure rebellious children, decent writers who are not published.

This dilemma is not new to the world. The Old Testament thinkers, Job's accusers among them, did their best to solve the problem. Unfortunately, they lacked assurance of the hereafter, so they tried to even up and tidy things here on earth. Common sense seemed to dictate that good people will be materially blessed and evil people punished. Unfortunately, this did not play in Job's hometown of Uz back in B.C., and it does not play in Peoria today. Ecclesiastes 8:14 says this:

> There is something else meaningless that occurs on earth: righteous men who get what the wicked deserve, and wicked men who get what the righteous deserve. This too, I say, is meaningless.

There is only one way to wring the cynicism out of this Scripture quotation, and indeed, out of the entire sad history of man straining to be good enough for God's blessings. That one sure way is grace. Jesus Christ is the "righteous man" pictured by Ecclesiastes who receives "what the wicked deserve." In so doing, Christ turns the common-sense rules about worthiness topsy-turvy.

In this marvelous, roundabout way, it is precisely our unworthiness that makes Christ real to us. Our complete situation of inability turns out to be our only consummate spiritual ability, for it causes us to trust solely in the cross. This is heavenly news concerning the worthiness hoop. Christ has firmly laid it aside. There is no need to vote on blame any longer. Whatever we have done, it has been forgiven. We are now newborns with no ugly past. We are finally free to face the present and the future with all of our faculties intact.

The only fly in the ointment is that we still live in the inexplicable Ecclesiastes world. At times, the righteous seem to get the bad things; at times, the unrighteous seem to get the good things. Christ begs us to understand this unmerited largess as a striking example of God's continuing goodness, the same reaching love that fashioned grace in the first place, "He causes his sun to rise on the evil and the good, and sends rain on the righteous and the unrighteous" (Matt. 5:45).

The bottom line is that our times of waiting are not penitential. All we can say is that the Wait is a complex, unpredictable snippet of earthly circumstances that we do not at present totally understand. Even if there has been a failure of character or of faith, grace has intervened. We have been made new, and we have no need to keep groveling in our dirty past to find that ultimate unconfessed fault that will finally open the heavenly floodgates. All we need is grace. "For it is by grace you have been saved, through faith—and this not from yourselves, it is the gift of God—not by works, so that no one can boast" (Eph. 2:8–9).

The Readiness Hoop

In our long, hard Wait, someone, somewhere, has tossed us this dried-up bone concerning our heart's desire: "It'll happen when you're ready." We obediently strain for the hoop, trying to live up to the person's general or specific ideals of "ready." What we do not see is that this is just a subtle shift in the blaming game. Instead of faulting our sins we fault our diligence.

Imagine this scene. The church is packed with wedding guests listening for the first whisper of the bride's petticoats. You are the father of the bride, gulping to rearrange your Adam's apple inside that tuxedo shirt with the meanly starched collar. Suddenly you are summoned to the parlor, told that your daughter is distraught and cannot possibly walk down the aisle until she has a word with you.

By the time you reach the parlor, you are itching with sweat. "What's wrong, sweetheart?" you croak, hoping she is not being taken ill.

"Oh, Daddy," she cries, "do you think I'm really ready to get married?"

Suddenly chills sweep all over your body. Not ready? Why, she is wearing a two-thousand-dollar, custom-made satin-and-pearl dress, and every gossiping soul from the office is sitting there on the pews, and over at the Hyatt in the lavish rented ballroom pink punch is spitting in a silverplated fountain! A fine time to be asking this question, you think. The collar oddly claws at your neck. What do you say?

Your first instinct is to dump a bucket of water on the fire, to soothe in your best fatherly tone by saying, "Oh, of course you're ready, honey. You're twenty-five years old. You're a college graduate, and you both have good jobs. Your groom is a wonderful fellow, and you two make such a great couple."

Your throat closes up. There is only one problem. It is a fairy tale. The bald and naked truth is that she is not ready. I mean, she is your little girl who never has dealt with a shady appliance repairman and who never has had to fight with a blanket hog on a frigid January night. Nothing has prepared her for the sight of her groom turned into a fatal whiner by his first violent stomach virus. And is her groom ready for his bride's purple-veined temper the first time he throws a wad of dirty socks on the kitchen table? And God forbid, she is not emotionally equipped yet for colicky babies and two A.M. feedings.

You clear your throat and give a squeaky but honest answer. "Sweetheart, none of us are ever really ready. But that's all right. We've all felt scared when we start out. We learn and grow as we go along."

Of course, sound preparation and maturity are potent ingredients for success. So are knowledge, experience, creativity, and flexibility. But none of those attributes are ever closed files. Rather, we keep them continually in process. That is why we need not become overburdened with our "unreadiness" and jump every time someone says "get ready . . . get set!" None of us can claim complete and thorough preparation for anything—parenthood, promotions, marriage, ministries. In fact, sometimes the best ministries are carried out by people who are not gifted, well bankrolled, or experienced. Such people, appreciating their lacks, rely more closely on God.

Is Peter ready for the arrest, crucifixion, and resurrection of his beloved Jesus? Of course not! Jesus predicts bluntly, "I tell you the truth, this very night, before the rooster crows, you will disown me three times" (Matt. 26:34). Yet, ready or not, Jesus has already declared his intention of using Peter as the rock on which his church is to be built. What could not be guessed at the time of Peter's failure is the later intervention and anointing of the Holy Spirit, which would rest fully on Peter and the others at Pentecost. Peter is indeed a rock and a saint under current construction, pending a walloping dose of power from on high.

Are we ready? Of course not. But that does not deter God. There are practical lessons we can gain only by living through the future for which we now hope. We should rely instead on the Holy Spirit. We will be surprised by what we can become on the very brink of the critical moment. "But you will receive power when the Holy Spirit comes on you" (Acts 1:8).

The Virtue-in-Waiting Hoop

We will recognize this hoop when someone says to us, "Oh, be patient and keep waiting. Your time will come. Good things come to those who wait." It feels right. I mean, we should have earned some consideration by virtue of the time we have put into waiting. While the worthiness hoop and the readiness hoop were based on false notions about our character, the virtue-in-waiting hoop centers on a false notion about the Wait itself. Let me illustrate by relating an experience with a killer line.

It was a sight to behold. There stood assembled every delinquent soul and every procrastinator in the county, at least two hundred strong, garbed in everything from business suits to flip-flops and curlers. Together we formed the car-tag line the day after the deadline. I hugged my four-month-old baby and trudged bravely to the end of the line, halfway around the block in the broiling sun.

At first I started out optimistically, like the good sport I try to be. I chatted with others in the line; I patta-caked with the baby; I quietly sang cheerful Brownie scout songs; I moved up quickly and obediently whenever the line budged.

But then my back began to complain. I leaned up against the wall. Ten percent better. I crouched down to a half sit. Thirty percent better. The line became sluggish; I became alarmed. Surely the ladies in the tag office would not be rude and inconsiderate enough to take a lunch break while I was out there waiting with an infant, of all things!

After about forty-five minutes, I knew I was on the verge. Frowns formed up and down the line over the baby's fussiness. Finally, a man saved my place while I walked the baby up and down the corridor we had now attained.

Baby feeding time rolled around. I knew then I was completely done in. I was nursing, and I was unable to leave for half an hour, and I certainly was unable to accomplish the task standing up in a public line. I jammed a pacifier into the hungry little mouth. With five hundred seven more jiggles and nineteen more perambulations I finally, blessedly, got inside the air conditioned glass doors.

But once inside the office, my heart turned to putty. There before me was a Chicago cattle stall of cordon ropes where at least fifty fellow refugees inched through the mazes. I was trapped, unable even to pace. Finally, I was called up to the window just as the baby was about to go belly up from sheer starvation.

And then it happened. This public servant behind the desk, who obviously knew nothing of what I had been through to attain her all-important station, flatly declared, "I'm sorry, but you don't have the proper documents."

I did the only imaginable thing. My throat swelled, and my eyes stung, and my face turned blotchy, and I outright blubbered, right there in front of the entire Department of Motor Vehicles. And, not to be outdone by his mother, so did the famished baby.

I thought I surely had earned a car tag. But it turned out that my heroic waiting in itself had no bearing on whether or not I got the tag. It all hinged on the documents I had failed to start out with way back at the very beginning of the ordeal.

Now I will finish the story by saying that some quick-thinking employee averted mass hysteria by hustling me off to an inner office where I could nurse the baby and get control of my sadly misplaced wits. Then I was introduced to another line where a computer operator could mysteriously find in the database the missing document number.

Of course, virtue can be gained in waiting, especially when it means we need not settle for a lesser choice when we may win the better choice through present self-denial and prudence. And indeed, interim times can be places of growth where positive things happen. In fact, that is the main premise of this book.

But waiting turns into a hoop-jumping exercise when we begin to see the time spent as a work-reward process, something like hours put in on a job. We think that if we wait long enough, we are more deserving of consideration than others who have not waited, or have not waited as long. Unfortunately, this fairness doctrine usually holds true for the ordinary wait but not for the Wait.

Jesus tells a parable that at first blush seems terribly unfair about a master who hires field hands at various times during the day and then pays each the same wage, starting with the last hired. Those who worked all day complain, thinking they are entitled to more. After all, they put in more time. The master replies, "Don't I have the right to do what I want with my own money? Or are you envious because I am generous?" (Matt. 20:15).

What most of us fail to realize is that in this story there was only one reward—a day's living. Nobody got more than that, nobody got less than that. In the car-tag line, only one item was offered—a car tag. It mattered not if I came in January and walked into an empty office and got a tag in two minutes or if I came in May and stood in line for two hours. All I could possibly ever leave with was a car tag. I received nothing extra for the length of the wait.

As an aside, those of us involved in the Wait should rejoice over this parable from Matthew. Think about the mental anguish of those last-hireds, sitting idly and helplessly in the dusty marketplace, sweating out whether or not they would eat that night. The first-hireds may have worked longer, but they did not suffer this terrible anxiety. One was occupied with work; one went through worry. It all evened out in the wash. The wage varied not.

So those who tell us that waiting in itself is virtuous are only selling pipe dreams. Our dream could come either right away or much later and still be the exact same dream. There is no intrinsic, ennobling value in waiting, nor any value in time itself spent doing anything apart from God. So if we have been working at waiting, now is the time to resign and find another job where the pay is better. Although certain time periods may seem unproductive, the generous master is able to reward both the work and the wait. Whether we have been actively harvesting from the beginning or have been waiting for employment until the last hour, the master graciously supplies us with the same coin of daily nurture.

Conclusion

If we happen to meet Mrs. Zophar during the Wait, remember that God says to the whole lot of Job's comforters, "You have not spoken about me what is right" (Job 42:7). The

Wait is tiring and draining enough without letting false notions turn it into a mental circus act. No one can explain to us why our dreams and prayers have been long delayed. There are no formulas we must follow, no mandatory lessons to master to coax open the heavenly floodgates.

Yes, we have many areas of our lives yet untilled by God's hand, but that does not change his love or generous desires for us. Yes, God may be teaching us and preparing us. But relax and let it be his work, not ours. That is why we call it grace. What hoops have we been needlessly jumping through?

Waiting Hungry

3

I once spoke with a woman named Trisha Gercken who was starved. We sat at her cozy oak table in her Jacksonville, Florida, kitchen with elbows planted on the quilted place mats, and over the hum of the fully laden refrigerator we descended together into the ugly depths of hunger. One by one Trisha's words straggled out, strung tight and bent in half in her throat.

Trisha told of the early days of optimism in the Wait when she had hoped for a baby who would have her husband Joe's wide, teasing grin or maybe Trisha's own liquid blue eyes. But months passed, and her longings grew for a baby that could be cradled in her needy arms. And, unfortunately, she chanced upon babies everywhere she went: the grocery store, church gatherings, even parking lots. Each unexpected encounter stirred up her emptiness, and there was nowhere she could hide from the painful onslaught.

One day on the way home from work Trisha drove past the local shopping center where a group of teenagers was set up for a charity car wash. Business was slow, so the teens were standing on the roadside waving magic-marker signs. Among the group was a ponytailed girl of perhaps twelve who added her own brand of exuberant showmanship to the advertisement by doing a cartwheel.

The girl was a nameless stranger to Trisha. But a salty, accusing voice taunted inside Trisha's head, "You'll probably never have a daughter to admire doing a cartwheel." Tears seared Trisha's eyes, and she was barely able to see to drive home. She was shaken and scared. Not only was she childless, her emotions were getting so out of hand that a mere glimpse of a twelve-year-old could slash open her emptiness like an infected wound. She was indeed waiting hungry.

Since by definition the Wait involves a crucial lifetime longing, the haughty specter of hunger can turn our lives into endless famine and constant emotional ambush. We desperately want and need something vital that we do not yet have.

Perhaps no one has ever objectively and compassionately talked to us about our hunger, most likely because there is no simple cure for such yearnings. Instead, our embarrassed corporate response has been to minimize the presence and importance of these emotionally hungry feelings. "Try putting your mind on something else. Just get busy doing something," we say. And in the awkward moments when emotion spills out and the raw reality cannot be sidestepped, we turn to mindless hen clucking, "There, there. As much as you want it, you'll appreciate it so much more when it finally gets here."

The first order of business in this chapter is to give healthy recognition to the validity of our hunger. It is terrible and it is real. It is not something that we have brought on ourselves, nor anything we should be able to whistle away. Enough busy work will not cure it, nor will any other substitute ever quite satisfy it. There is absolutely nothing we or anyone else can tell inner hunger that will make it go away. Pretending inner hunger can be ordered away is as foolish as using mere words to remedy physical hunger (see James 2:15–16).

Hunger does not negate our faith. Neither is it a symptom of ingratitude for our many other blessings. Inner hunger- ings are a natural part of having dreams and hopes, being human, living on earth time, and awaiting positive change. So we will grant ourselves permission to be unapologetically starved. During the Wait we cannot help but be anything else.

Hunger the Taskmaster

We begin with a huge problem. Waiting is torture enough, but waiting hungry is ten times worse. Through unpleasant experience, every auto repair shop manager in America knows how irritable hungry customers can become. No won- der the plastic seats in the waiting area face dead center into snack and soft drink vending machines. But inner hunger is different. At times "feed me" screams so loudly inside of our heads that we will settle for any makeshift remedy at all fool- ish costs. At those times we are in danger of letting hunger become our unkind taskmaster.

As an illustration, let me introduce someone I call June. June suffers from sensitivities to manmade elements. All syn- thetics, plastics, and chemicals seem to affect her immune system. She spent one whole summer sleeping in a canvas tent when her house was sprayed by an exterminator. Today she is back under a roof where walls are unpainted, carpets have been torn out, and nearly every stick of furniture has been given away. June cannot socialize; she cannot work; she cannot even read because the chemicals in the print cause her head to swim. June's life has been stripped.

No physician in the state has been able to help June. June has tried health food, pills, vitamins, healing services, envi- ronmental control, rest, exercise, support groups, counseling, and alternative medicine. No wonder June is so desperate to get well that she will try anything.

One day I accompanied June to the latest "therapy" at a clinic on a quiet, residential street in an urban area. There I got a scary glimpse of life in a hunger-driven world. I use the term *clinic* generously. It was a 1930s brick bungalow with no identifying sign and, most likely, no business license. The only way the place was known was through word of mouth on the alternative-treatment grapevine.

Before we go on, let me say that I applaud June's determination and attempts toward wellness. June is a valued friend, and I accompanied her because I wanted to support her in her quest for wellness. During our trip that day I simply drew the conclusion that this particular treatment was not on the up-and-up.

Since the treatment room (former bedroom) in this "clinic" was expediently off-limits to nonpatients, I have only a vague description of a computer system of German gadgetry which purportedly diagnoses diseases without so much as drawing a drop of blood. It was claimed that this machine could even go so far as to uncover accurately the shadows of diseases still present in your body that have been passed down from your grandparents. I found this an interesting claim, since most grandparents are dead and unable to verify or deny such claims. Even those still alive could never disprove that some "palsy" or "vapor" they suffered in their younger days was not, in fact, the very disease the computer indicated.

In the waiting room/living room, I met another acutely health-needy couple who had driven over from Alabama expressly for this treatment. They had made the six-hour drive and would wait several more hours to be squeezed in. It was obvious that they believed in this wizardry and anything else that offered hope, including the notion that oregano in large enough amounts can cure cancer.

Unfortunately the "therapist" was unable to help June that day. This was blamed on an infected tooth which had to be extracted before the treatments would work. June was allowed to buy some "supplements" which were huge, white, refrigerated pills whose main ingredient sounded like human breast milk. June subsequently had a dentist extract the tooth in question, but soon afterward the "therapist" moved on to another city. June was left with a hole in her gums, still suffering from her environmental illness.

I left that day knowing that I had been admitted into the harsh shadow lands of the Wait. June and the Oregano Couple had become victims of hunger the taskmaster. Out of their compelling need they had sought help, listened desperately for any word of hope, and then counted out their cash to someone offering them even the most remote chance of relief. All of this is very old news. June and the Oregano Couple are modern-day examples of the biblical sufferer who touched the cloak of Jesus. It can indeed be said today as it was back then: No one had been able to cure her (Luke 8:43).

June's treatment story seems less extreme when we compare it with our own acute feelings of need. During the Wait not only does hunger make us miserable, but it also sets us up for exploitation. Opportunists take advantage of lonely people; charlatans take in ill people; profit-minded employers underpay and overwork people who long for career advancement and recognition. Con artists prey on people with financial problems; cult groups thrive on people awaiting affirmation. Cycles of abuse and exploitation can even go on in the most intimate of relationships—between spouses or between parent and child. Not to be outdone, the mass media targets our emptiness as a sure means of profit, pitching products aimed at filling our "needs," even if the "needs" have to be overinflated or invented.

Jesus was well acquainted with inner hunger. His longings were more terrible than ours could ever be, for he hungered for a wayward and troubled people to know the Father. Jesus said, "I have come to bring fire on the earth, and how I wish it were already kindled! But I have a baptism to undergo, and how distressed I am until it is completed" (Luke 12:49–50)! In place of the word *distressed*, the KJV uses the word *straitened*, which means subjected to distress and deficiency or deprived of the very elements needed for existence.

The temptations of Christ in the wilderness involve both physical and mental hunger. Although Jesus masters hunger during this first go-around, the taskmaster is far from through with him, always goading him throughout his ministry to show a sign, work a decisive miracle, seize the wrong hour, grab the worldly throne by military force, take the easy road, preserve his own life, or bow down to political expediency. Jesus does none of these things.

Christ's first meeting with the taskmaster takes place after his baptism when the Spirit leads him into the wilderness. There Jesus prays and fasts for forty days. The Bible says, "He ate nothing during those days, and at the end of them he was hungry" (Luke 4:2). After forty days without food, no wonder Jesus is a prime target for attack; no wonder the taskmaster appears. The Bible, of course, calls the taskmaster the devil and does not even dignify him with a capitalized title.

The wilderness is a rocky spot, and I can imagine that the devil needs to use very little power of suggestion for the brown, jagged rocks to start looking like bread crusts to Jesus. "They're nearly bread already," the devil whispers. "Just turn one into bread for real. Go ahead, put it up to your mouth. You're going to die if you don't eat, and what good are you to God, then? If you're really his son, you can do it. It's child's play."

The devil is, in effect, asking Christ to satisfy his hunger at all costs. Christ answers firmly, "Man does not live on bread alone" (Luke 4:4).

We usually imagine this scene dispassionately. A haloed Christ is standing upright, one hand pointing declaratively toward heaven, preaching Scripture to the devil. I think not. Christ is bent over his ravenous stomach, his head is pounding, and he can hardly see straight. His skin is sunburnt, his hair is tangled, and his tongue feels like old shoe leather. Christ makes no false pretense about not being hungry. He does not say, "Thanks anyway, but I'll just grab a bite later on." Such pretending does not work with the devil. The devil has hunger radar.

Christ's answer instead puts the situation into a larger framework. Too often we miss seeing the framework; we only see the small nail of Scripture on which Christ hangs it. At those give-it-to-me-quickly times we want the quotation itself to be the silver bullet that will kill the evil vampire hunger. We must soberly remember that primly mouthing Scriptures is not a magical antidote to temptation. In this same scene, the devil himself sweetly and ably quotes from the Bible.

The Scripture defines and declares the context of Christ's life as a whole, including what he is going to do about this urgent life-consuming hunger. He is going to rely on God. Although the "bread alone" quotation is short, it is permeated with forty years' worth of wisdom gleaned by Moses from his own wilderness wanderings. Moses says in Deuteronomy, "He humbled you, causing you to hunger and then feeding you with manna, which neither you nor your fathers had known, to teach you that man does not live on bread alone but on every word that comes from the mouth of the Lord" (Deut. 8:3).

Jesus says in effect to the devil, "No loaf of bread, no matter how badly needed, is worth more than the baker." If filling our emptiness takes our eyes off God as our provider, then it is much better to remain hungry for now, as difficult and life threatening as that seems.

To be sure, it is extremely hard to keep actions rational and sound while that empty place in our belly is making insane cries and protests. We must intimately know and trust God our provider before hunger strikes. We must resolve beforehand to use extreme and utter caution when considering possible remedies for our hunger.

One way to do this is to question the reliability and motivation of the source of the proffered answer, especially when someone offers a quick and painless fix. We need to keep ourselves under the protection offered by loving family, friends, and Christian community. We need to listen when our trusted friends offer an honest evaluation of our proposed hunger remedy. Once in touch with this trusted objectivity, we should continue to question: Is this the best means of help? Is the person offering this remedy in a position to profit from it? Does this person offering relief genuinely care about me?

Finally, we should entertain a straightforward question that perhaps has not even occurred to us before. Is hunger all bad? Such questions are seldom asked in a consumer society where solutions routinely must be researched, invented, manufactured, and marketed for every problem, big or small, including dandruff. Perhaps this fire in our belly instead could be a positive force, a motivator, a holy restlessness, an edge that keeps us moving outward until we stretch and grow into a surprisingly distant place where God is leading.

Hunger the Friend

As a struggling writer I had the chance to meet Elizabeth Sherrill, a writer and editor whose work I often had admired. In the hallway during a break at a workshop, I asked her haltingly, "What do you think my chances are of having a book published?"

She looked at me squarely and proclaimed, "You're a good writer, Karen. I'm sure you'll be published."

Two years later I was again with Elizabeth at a workshop. Unfortunately, I was still unpublished. At dinner another writer was telling Elizabeth how important her modest writing earnings were to the family income. I remarked that my husband earned a comfortable income and, luckily, my writings did not have to earn their keep.

Elizabeth's next comment caused me pause. "Now, I'm a bit worried about you, Karen. Those who must earn money from writing to pay the bills learn to please the editors and help the audience and not themselves. Otherwise you spend your time on pet projects."

I never had stopped to think of the stagnation and complacency that sometimes results when we try to domesticate and minimize our hunger. I returned home and sat honestly before God, unfolding my unpublished writing projects, letting the truth of Elizabeth's declaration sink in. I prayed something that might sound quite strange in view of this discussion on hunger the taskmaster. I actually closed my eyes and whispered, "God, make me hungrier."

I made that petition not because I wanted a taskmaster but because I needed a helpful friend. My petition was about getting back in touch with my natural yearnings. I stopped pretending that it was all right if my writings did not sell; I stopped hiding behind the excuse that it was not important because the money was not important. I instead admitted that rejection hurt. Rejection hurt because I longed to be heard. God had put something that stirred restlessly inside of me, compelling me to write. The force was hunger, but it was positive energy, sending me back time and time again to try to wrap truths into words that could be understood.

Hunger the friend can motivate us not only to try new things, but it can sustain us through difficulties, engender love in our hearts for others in distress, and fit us for newfound ministry.

To illustrate hunger's monumental helpful power, I will continue Trisha's story of infertility that began this chapter. Trisha's relationship with God began to change, not by her being sweetly satisfied but by her being stretched, questioned, and challenged. One day when she again had been told she had failed to conceive, she yelled out loud at God in a medical building parking garage, "Where are you? Haven't you been listening?" Whatever else, her communication with God became honest, real, and daily, not all dressed up, pretend, and saved for Sunday morning.

Trisha's acute emotions motivated her to seek out medical treatment. One day she chanced to hear a radio talk show on infertility and learned about the medical specialty of reproductive endocrinology. She immediately made an appointment. When the doctor suggested major exploratory abdominal surgery, Trisha agreed. Her hunger had provided her with the courage to face productive pain.

At the same time her growing faith gave her the resources to deal with the possible discovery of inoperable barrenness. Right before the surgery she wrote in a poem to God, "I'll accept the results of this surgery as your word to me, whether you want me to have my own child or to love one that you've already sent to somebody else."

Two months after the surgery, Trisha was pregnant. Although her Wait of infertility was over, hunger's work was not yet finished. Longing and hope had to continue to simmer within to sustain Trisha's resolve when her pregnancy turned out to be a medical nightmare. One horrible day she suffered a miscarriage. It seemed a miserable end to her happy hopes. In a bizarre series of events a sonogram revealed that she indeed had lost a baby but had been carrying twins, and one tiny peanut of an embryo was still clinging to life within her womb. Next, a growth developed on Trisha's ovary. At five months, the tumor grew large enough to imperil the baby's growth. In a risky operation, Trisha's womb was lifted from her abdomen, and the tumor hastily was removed.

Trisha and her unborn baby recovered from this ordeal only to experience more threats: a ruptured incision, toxemia, and gestational diabetes. A person less hungry might have been done in, but Trisha felt that she was carrying a miracle baby. Whatever the outcome, the child would always be an answer to long-seeking prayer. Trisha's daughter, Erica Faith, arrived amidst the same medical drama that had characterized her conception and gestation. On October fifth, Erica was born in an emergency midnight cesarean.

If we return to our original kitchen-table talk with Trisha where she described so graphically her gnawing hunger, we will be surprised to notice new details I did not include in the opening scene. Right next to the table is a high chair with a dirty bib, and in the dish drainer over by the refrigerator are newly washed baby bottles. And there, just now learning to pull herself up as her soft, pink hands journey up her mother's knees, is healthy, happy, one-year-old Erica.

Although Trisha has finished her Wait, the experience was still useful. She reopened the feelings for me as a witness and a help for others. She said that she had been emotionally supporting an infertile friend. Trisha could not give her friend a child, but Trisha could give her the gift of sympathetic understanding and encouragement.

So we end in the company of hunger the friend instead of hunger the taskmaster. Once-hungry but now-filled people see longing in others, and instead of seeking to exploit this hunger, they feel overflowing hearts of empathetic, yearning love. It brings out the best in them, evokes self-giving without thought of repayment, gives them the courage to reenter their own pain to lessen that of another.

Christ reaches back into his own wilderness hunger when his tired eyes survey the crowd camped out in a lonely place to hear his message (see Mark 8). Three days have consumed their meager rations, and now journeying homeward on foot without a meal might cause some to faint. Jesus and his disciples quietly go about feeding them—all four thousand—with just seven loaves and one fish.

How on earth could so many have been fed on so little? The act defies explanation. Jesus proposes feeding them, and the people obediently sit down to receive whatever food he might offer. Perhaps their quiet trust is as great a miracle as the multiplied bread. Maybe this is the true cause of Christ's prayer of thanksgiving. Could he have prayed as he looked out over the stilled, expectant hillside, "God, four thousand of your children are hungry today. Yet they've chosen to stay in this lonely place with you rather than to go off and try to provide for themselves. Their hunger is real, but they now know that you are just as real, as present as their constant need for food. From this moment forward, they no longer live on bread alone. They live by every filling word you have to say to them."

The disciples distribute the rations, and everyone eats and has enough. The hardened stones of survivalist thinking have at last been turned into the soft, nourishing bread of trust.

Conclusion

We recognize hunger as our long-term, inescapable condition in the Wait. We must continually cope with the pain and vulnerability it hands us while we try to maintain objectivity. In the end, we can allow God to use hunger as our friend, motivator, and means of outreaching care.

Jesus says, "Blessed are they which do hunger and thirst after righteousness: for they shall be filled (Matt. 5:6 KJV). What would happen if we dared to make friends with our hunger?

Putting on Life's
4
Sombrero

One rainy October morning as I drove to the country home of songwriter Tricia Steedley Cudd, who lives in Clyde, North Carolina, I thought I was embarking on a routine interview. As I look back over my journals, I now see that, instead, I was being initiated into a way of life that would mean my own survival half a year later in one of the most traumatic disappointments of my own Wait.

As I got out of my car, I shooed the curious pet chickens of various pedigrees from my path, and I couldn't help gawking at the carport rafters draped with white blinking Christmas lights. Tricia came out in response to the stirring animals and answered my unvoiced surprise about the unseasonable lights. "The lights are to remind the children in my music and art program that they're each a special light for Jesus and that they can reach for the stars."

Tricia's slight, girl-like figure was wrapped in a long cotton dress. Her shoulders were thin, and her hair, dark and long, fell loosely around her neck. She told me that her grandmother was a Cherokee Indian, and indeed Tricia's eyes were nearly black, peering out from behind round, wire-rimmed glasses.

We passed through the carport into a former garage that was now Tricia's studio and the site of her children's music and art program. The garage was full of big, dark amplifiers, innumerable tubes of paint that had been squeezed every imaginable direction, tambourines, guitars, costumes, a potter's wheel, and globby little pieces of clay sculptures drying in puddles.

Tricia placed in my hand a small, round ball of hard clay that had been painted yellow and then marked with a smiley face. Oddly enough, there was a whole box of them. "Here," she pronounced, "have a giggle. I give them away, and when you hold them, you're supposed to laugh and smile."

Tricia then offered me a seat on a bright-red, wooden, child's chair saying, "God just gave me another song. I've written over two hundred. Would you like for me to sing it? You'll be the very first one to ever hear it."

I nodded. As she turned to pick up her twelve-string guitar, she noticed a large sombrero on the counter. This was no ordinary hat. It was at least four feet wide, so heavy that the sides drooped and sat on the wearer's shoulders. It was more like an umbrella or a raffia cape than a hat. "Would you like to wear a sombrero while you listen?" she asked as if she were offering me a cup of tea.

I shook my head, suddenly feeling self-conscious, unprofessional, and all knees in the miniature chair. A cat and a dog vied for squatter's rights against my ankles. Tricia barely took notice. She began to sing words from a notebook on her lap, using amplifiers and microphones just for me, an audience of one.

The guitar music was masterful and hypnotizing, but it was Tricia's voice that caught me by surprise. I had expected something operatic, but Tricia's voice was unadorned and humble, with a range that did not go quite as low as she sometimes tried to make it. It was a folk singer's voice, filled with timbre, pathos of heart, and simple feeling, unconscious of anything but the thread of the song winding itself out of her soul.

There I sat, knees in the air, listening to a newborn song, not sure what to think of Tricia or myself, nagged by a spoiling thought about how silly I would look in a sombrero and about how Tricia's voice failed to hit the occasional low note.

As these warring feelings still lingered inside of me, the guitar strings stilled, and Tricia told me about the Wait. Tricia's Wait was about affirmation, and it had taken her whole life through her mid-thirties. Her childhood had been less than ideal. Dreams and accomplishments had been few, education minimal.

Tricia's father worked in a paperboard factory and was not a totally reliable family man. Once he took all of the money out of the savings account and ran off for four months with the family car. Tricia's mother made do with her unsatisfactory marital lot, but it slowly robbed her of all warmth and optimism. Thin, awkward, and timid, Tricia received few encouraging words about her self-worth. But Tricia had one small hope. She loved music. She imagined herself onstage, bowing to receive warm applause. When Tricia was seven years old, she cut a guitar shape out of paperboard and did her best to string it with rubber band strings. Her father saw Tricia and asked, "What on earth are you going to do with that thing?"

Tricia replied quietly, "I'm going to sing my songs to the world."

"Well," her father replied with a laugh, "to do that, you're going to need real strings." He went out and bought guitar strings and tightened them onto a wooden block on the cardboard. That cardboard guitar became a treasure to Tricia. In fact, as she told the story, she showed the very cardboard guitar to me, twenty-five years later, hanging there on her studio garage wall.

Tricia's father gave her a real guitar when she turned sixteen, and Tricia taught herself to play as she continued her long quest for positive affirmation. She married at age seventeen to escape her dismal home life, and, as sometimes happens in such hasty marriages, she soon divorced. She married again, began raising two daughters, and joined a church where she found a niche as a volunteer children's song leader. Tricia was by then an accomplished guitar player, but she was still so unsure of herself that she would not sing alone, even in front of a group of children. Instead, she always chose a child with a good voice to stand beside her.

When Tricia was nearly thirty, her father was diagnosed with terminal cancer. During the last weeks of his life he called Tricia to his bedside and whispered, "Please forgive me for all the wrong I've done you."

Tears rolled down Tricia's cheeks, and she replied, "Of course I forgive you, Daddy. I love you."

It might have been Tricia's long-awaited moment, but it was stolen away in the hospital lobby on her father's final trip home. Tricia's mother was pushing the wheelchair, and the oxygen tank began to fall. Tricia said matter-of-factly, "Mom, be careful."

Tricia's mother straightened up. With a cold, irrational glint in her eye, she slapped Tricia on the face and hissed, "Just leave us alone, you Jezebel!"

Tricia was shocked. What on earth had prompted the slap? Only years later would Tricia understand that her mother saw Tricia's mended relationship with her father as traitorous. Tricia's forgiveness had been so total and genuine that the man died in peace, his eyes set on heaven, and not the hell Tricia's mother felt he had slowly but surely fashioned for himself.

Tricia entered one of the darkest times of her life, not knowing what she had done to so terribly displease her mother. Tricia waited for things to blow over with her mom: one year, two, three, four. Her mother continued her silent neglect, having little contact with Tricia beyond that of a polite stranger.

In this setting something else happened that might have been taken in stride if Tricia had not already been broken down under the Wait. Tricia received a letter from the church asking her to resign from her volunteer music job. Tricia was rattled down to the core of her being. Music was her life. Over a two-month period she begged for reconsideration. Finally, one Sunday the minister gave her a final and unequivocal no. The church did not want her music. It was dead.

The very next day Tricia bent to put a log in the wood-burning stove, and a searing pain flashed down her spine. She collapsed and lay in agony for several hours until she could pull herself to the sofa. She began physical therapy, but her pain got no better. Her eyes swam, and her feet often went numb and folded under her. She could no longer keep house or take care of her children. She descended into utter blackness.

One morning as she was clinging in pain to her kitchen sink, the sun suddenly broke through a cloud. The oddest thing happened. A song went through Tricia's mind, one she had never heard before. She groped her way back to the bedroom and picked up her guitar. The song was about a very sad person looking for hope. The person in the song needed a breakthrough, something as unmistakable as the morning clouds parting to admit the sun into her kitchen window.

Tricia's continual decline finally brought her to a neurosurgeon's office. After running tests, the doctor told Tricia that she had been born with spina bifida occulta and had suffered a severe muscular sprain. Then he stopped talking about physical conditions and asked Tricia about her parents.

Tricia thought it an odd question, but the doctor patiently listened as Tricia haltingly told the sad story of her father's death. Finally, the doctor said, "Tricia, when I look at you, I don't see any spark. It's like somebody's turned off your inner light. Your father supported your music, and now he's gone. God put a spark inside all of us. It's up to you to make it come back on. If you could try just one thing that would make you happy, one thing that you were born to do, what would it be?"

Tricia felt the answer leap out of her heart. She realized that she was, indeed, the very sad person in the song she had composed that day by the kitchen sink. "Music," she answered softly.

The doctor wrote out a few words on his prescription pad and tore off the sheet for Tricia. There were no medicinal codes on the slip. It instead read, "Sing your songs to the world."

Tricia took the doctor's advice, and there I sat that rainy October day in her garage-turned-into-a-studio. She had found a small church that welcomed her songs; she had started a music and art class for children. Her inner light was now shining, and her back had slowly gotten better one day at a time. Best of all, Tricia was now a musician. She was indeed singing her songs to the world.

Tricia was not a musician because someone bought a tape or bragged about her talent. She was not a musician because she had earned a lot of money or won an award or filled an auditorium. She was a musician because she was brave enough to make music for herself, to create simply for the sake of creating, because that was what she was born to do. She had finally discovered that we do not have to wait for affirmation. It can be God-given and can come from the inside, even if it never comes from the outside.

I sat transfixed. It was there at the end of Tricia's story that I suddenly regretted not putting on the sombrero. What I had been offered was a wonderful gift of self-forgetfulness. I had been so busy making myself conform to the image of a successful, businesslike writer that I had lost the chance of fully enjoying the process.

I suddenly grasped Tricia's secret. It was receptivity. Tricia's songs came because she let them come, each one delightful and newborn, wet and shiny, ready to be heard and enjoyed without thought for formal rendering in musical notations. She had allowed the years to fall away to recapture the childlike joy that is inside of each one of us, the delight that dances and giggles. She had regained the ability to create without constraint, without worrying that what was created would pass the worthiness test in the eye of any other beholder.

Now Tricia's whole world was full of joy impractical. On the cluttered kitchen counter where the dish drainer should have been was an institutional-sized glass jar with black clam shells sunk on the bottom and two large frilly goldfish swimming around. On the back porch was an old-fashioned wringer washer, used for the family wash because "it just feels right." This same porch had a tin roof that sounded "right" in the October rain.

Tricia's bathroom was full of sock monkeys hanging from the shower curtain bar and perched by the sink. She even had a "dressing room." It was really a small bedroom with clothes racks, an ironing board, and a small, mirrored vanity table dripping with costume jewelry and baubles like a pirate's chest. The walls were festooned with garments—tiny, puffed-sleeve dresses long outgrown, evening wear long since outdated, even a toddler's bikini.

I was finally experiencing Tricia's world, and I felt the abundance of it all. It was a lush world, totally different from the hungry worlds to which I had journeyed in the Wait. It was a king-sized world, full of things that pleased the soul. But oddly enough, nothing was costly. It was simply clay giggles that could be held in the hand, goldfish to converse with on the kitchen counter, clothes squeezed through a wringer while she listened to rain dancing on a tin roof.

Despite the Wait, Tricia had learned to live a supernatural life. She was abiding in the joy of Psalm 24:1: "The earth is the LORD's, and everything in it, the world, and all who live in it."

Putting on the Sombrero

One thing all of our Waits have in common is something of Tricia's struggle to become. There is an element of fighting against that which we cannot yet claim to be, a search for affirmation from somewhere outside ourselves. Could putting on the sombrero now change how we wait?

Putting on life's sombrero embodies many things. It means not fretting about becoming accomplished; it involves letting ourselves try new things while giving ourselves permission to make honest mistakes. Slowly we come to the place where we can enjoy the ongoing process rather than set our sights solely on the final product. Self-affirmation in effect means laying aside perfectionism and relishing instead the rollicking journey of discovery and growth.

Putting on life's sombrero also means redefining ourselves. It takes a certain amount of fearlessness to carve out our own definition of who we are, listening to what God says about our worth and not what the world has to say. It also takes courage to lose self-consciousness, to become again childlike, humble, and teachable. Perhaps this is what Jesus means when he says, "Let the little children come to me, and do not hinder them, for the kingdom of God belongs to such as these. I tell you the truth, anyone who will not receive the kingdom of God like a little child will never enter it" (Mark 10:14–15).

We might easily give a nodding assent to all of these thoughts about life's sombrero. However, understanding a truth and acting on it are two entirely different matters. I personally did not put on the sombrero for three months after my visit with Tricia. Oddly enough, I was not conscious of doing so until the very moment I had done it.

January 25 was just an ordinary morning of everyday work. I sat down at my computer to work on a novel that I had put on the back burner during Christmas. Suddenly, out of nowhere, the joy was inexplicably there. I wrote in my journal, "I was born to do this. I am a novelist. I can do it. It feels solid and good and right and powerful. I've been waiting all of this time for a book contract that says, 'You're a novelist.' But the fact is, I *am* a novelist."

Please listen carefully. This is something quite different from the power of positive thinking. I was not picturing myself as something I hoped to be, conjuring up an image of the future so strong and undeniable that it absolutely had to happen. On the contrary, I was finally allowing myself to admit what I was already about. It was not a saccharin, some-day dream. It was a bold-faced risk about today. The risk was in declaring my own satisfaction with my progress even when others might deem me a failure or a hopeless dreamer.

The fact is, the dictionary definition of a novelist says simply "a writer of novels." The hesitancy was not in what I was doing but rather in the arena of public opinion and acclaim. Yes, it continued to be quite embarrassing in casual conversation to mention that I was a novelist and then to admit that no, I did not have a publisher. But that discomfort was not about my work; it was about my ideas of worldly success.

Meditate on this for a moment. What is the true reason we have not yet accepted affirmation for something that we already are becoming? Is it because we might feel foolish if others fail to affirm it? If so, we really are awaiting acclaim, not affirmation. The real tension, then, is not about outer event but rather about fear, self-protection, and face-saving.

The mind-boggling part of all of this is that outer event does not necessarily bring inner peace. We all have read interviews of successful entertainers living in million-dollar homes who still do not feel they have made it. The bottom line is that we, too, might possibly finally receive the very thing we have long awaited only to find that the accolades were not the remedy we needed after all. All along, the fight was not against unwieldy circumstance but against self-doubt.

Although this principle of affirmation at first seems to fit best into Waits about long-sought accomplishments, it applies in some degree to all Waits. In the case of someone awaiting the return of a wayward child, the turning about of the child is the outer, future event. However, in the meantime, inside the parent is a gnawing feeling of inadequacy. The parent might think, "Because my child is in such rebellion, I must not be a good parent. I must have done something dreadfully wrong." That, indeed, is the societal yardstick, the worldly accolade. If our children turn out well, we get pats on the back as being good and successful parents, whether or not we had much to do with it.

Now sometime in the distant future, at age twenty-eight or thirty-eight, this wayward child might say, "You know, Mom and Dad, you were right all of those years. Thanks for hanging in there for me." But the fact is, these parents today at this very moment, are hanging in there for this child. That is why they have every right to put on the sombrero today. The heartbreaking anguish they now feel points up the fact that they are the very best of parents, wounded by deep and reaching love. This is the epitome of love, biblical and God-like (see Isa. 49:15–16).

In the same way, one can indeed be a good spouse even though divorced, a worthy marriage partner even while remaining single, a nurturing and giving person while childless, a strong and mentally healthy person while mortally ill. One can also be a person rich in joy and friends while bankrupt, an excellent employee with marketable skills while continuing to be unemployed. It is possible to be a person of consummate joy and worth, during the Wait and despite the Wait.

Accepting God's Affirmation

Unfortunately, once we decide to put on life's sombrero, it easily can be knocked off. During the Wait there are many gusts of wind with force enough to carry off even the best-fitting hat.

The assailing wind does not necessarily have to be a catastrophe. It just as easily can be a single discouraging comment, a hopeless mood, or even long, dull, dreary weariness.

My sombrero did not stay on very long. A rejection knocked it off on March 19. On that day the novel that bore my high hopes was returned with a short businesslike note. I wallowed around in self-pity. Not only that, but I went around hatless for three months. Then, on June 16, still very depressed over my misfortune, I lay fitfully in bed. I found myself making a little pleading prayer, "God, I love doing this [writing novels] so much . . . please . . . please . . ."

Just as I whimpered that little mental plea, a thought struck me: *What am I crying out about? God loves my writing; God wants me to write. It's done in heaven. Does it matter if it isn't done on earth? His perfect will for me is the joy that I feel in writing. Does it matter that economic or market conditions may never open up for me? I thought of the phrase "on earth as it is in heaven," and suddenly it made sublime sense to me. Isn't heaven indeed a place free from the constraints of human boundaries* (see Matt. 6:10)?

It suddenly seemed foolish to plead with God about my dreams. He believed in my dreams. He put me together and gave me those dreams. What God brought to my attention that June night was Scripture. It is the only way to tie on a hat against the wind. The next morning I got out the concordance and the dictionary and looked up the word *delight*. The dictionary describes delight as a high degree of gratification, great joy, and extreme satisfaction.

Here is the foremost Scripture passage that describes how God feels about us, "For the Lord will take delight in you, and your land will be married. As a young man marries a maiden, so will your sons marry you; as a bridegroom rejoices over his bride, so will your God rejoice over you" (Isa. 62:4–5).

As I listened to Tricia's songs again, I finally understood that her ability to affirm herself came from what God has to say about who she is in Christ. One of her most powerful songs is entitled, "I Am." The song is a mind-boggling 186 stanzas long and lists who God says we are. Here are some selected parts:

> I'm an overcomer
> More than a conqueror
> I've been made new
> I'm the apple of his eye.

> I'm a difference maker
> A victory taker
> I'm a hand raiser
> I'm holding them up to the Lord above
> I'm a partaker of his love.

> I am a treasure
> Jesus takes pleasure
> When I am doing the things He's shown
> His love is the greatest ever known.

> I am a dwelling place
> I walk in a joyous pace
> Not being moved by what I see
> There is a great God inside of me.

Tricia ends her song by saying, "I am . . . an overcomer." I took the challenge of looking up every stanza and found a Scripture reference to back up every one. For instance, God does indeed call us a treasure in the King James Version of Exodus 19:5: "Now therefore, if ye will obey my voice indeed, and keep my covenant, then ye shall be a peculiar treasure unto me above all people: for all the earth is mine." Here are the stanzas to Tricia's song again with their biblical references:

> I'm an overcomer: 1 John 5:4
> More than a conqueror: Rom. 8:37
> I've been made new: Rev. 21:5
> I'm the apple of his eye: Deut. 32:10

I'm a difference maker: Matt. 5:14
A victory taker: 1 Cor. 15:57
I'm a hand raiser: Ps. 134:2
I'm holding them up to the Lord above: Ps. 63:4
I'm a partaker of his love: 1 John 3:1

I am a treasure
Jesus takes pleasure
When I am doing the things he's shown: Exod. 19:5
His love is the greatest ever known: John 15:13

I am a dwelling place: Ps. 90:1
I walk in a joyous pace: Col. 1:10–11
Not being moved by what I see: 2 Cor. 5:7
There is a great God inside of me: John 14:17

Accepting self-affirmation and God's affirmation of us are distinct events that happen over and over again. What God has to say about us gives us confidence and courage; our confidence and courage can be permanently in place only when they are anchored firmly in God.

Accepting the Yellow Bowl

Tricia had one more unforgettable lesson to teach me about affirmation. Her story continues with an account of her mother's death. Five years after the death of Tricia's father and just half a year after Tricia began singing again, her mother was diagnosed with terminal breast cancer. It was February, her mom's birthday was coming up, and Tricia had no money for a gift. Worst of all, there still had been no words of reconciliation.

At the same time, Tricia was trying to decide on a theme for her next children's music class, when a strange thought came into her mind: snow. Now, snow is an extreme rarity in South Carolina where Tricia lived at the time, and the daffodils were already poking out of the ground. Tricia nevertheless went to work collecting and duplicating songs about snow.

Afterward the inner voice said, "Tell the children it's going to snow." [In a later chapter we shall investigate the inner voice more thoroughly.] In even this small matter, Tricia obeyed. On Friday afternoon she told the children in her class, "I want everybody to make a snowman and make a picture of it for me." Then she bowed her head and thanked God for the snow he would send.

On Saturday night the one and only snowfall of the winter arrived. Tricia heard the inner voice again, which said, "Get a big bag of snow and put it in the freezer." She went to the middle of a field and harvested the fluffiest, purest snow.

By Thursday the snow had dissolved into dreary mud, and Tricia set out to drive the hundred miles to visit her mother, still without a gift. Her mother was propped up in the living room, wearing a gray stocking cap pulled down over her head to hide the ravages of chemotherapy. Tricia said haltingly, "You look like you're ready for snow. We had the most beautiful snow last week."

Her mother simply stared, but Tricia's Aunt Mamie shook her head sadly. "We were hoping for snow but didn't get any. Your mom was saying the other day if she could have just one thing before she died, it would be a big bowl of snow cream. The chemotherapy makes everything taste so bad."

A surge of recognition went through Tricia. "I'm coming back next week, Mom, and I'm bringing your birthday present. I've got a big bag of snow in my freezer."

Her mother shook her head dolefully. "It'll melt."

"Not this snow," Tricia replied. "This is miracle snow."

The next weekend Tricia packed the snow from her freezer into a ten-gallon cooler and wrapped it in a quilt. When she arrived, none of the snow had melted. The snow was like sudden magic, turning the solemn assembly of relatives into a party as they pinched off snow to melt on their tongues. Tricia passed out the song sheets, and the little living room was filled with the singing of snow songs. Finally, Tricia turned to her mother and asked, "Do you still have that big yellow bowl, the one you always made snow cream in when I was little?"

Her mom gave a puzzled shake of her head, but Aunt Mamie jumped up. "I know exactly where it is." Tricia followed her aunt into the kitchen. Aunt Mamie climbed onto the counter to reach the top kitchen cabinet and handed Tricia a yellow glass bowl with a creamy white interior saying, "I'll get out the ingredients. You make it."

Tricia made the snow cream, put some into a small bowl, and gave it to her mother. As Tricia sang "Happy Birthday," her mother took a bite of the snow cream and let it melt on her lips. She nodded. "Mmm. This is the best snow cream I've ever had."

A month later, Tricia's mother died. There was never the kind of reconciliation that Tricia had enjoyed with her father. Her mother's last will and testament read, "Although I acknowledge Tricia as my daughter, I leave her nothing."

This final rebuff was nearly a mortal blow to Tricia. She stood for the last time in the little hallway of her mother's house, crying miserably. Finally, she looked up and saw Aunt Mamie standing in the doorway to the kitchen. Aunt Mamie had the big yellow bowl cradled to her bosom. She took two little steps and pulled Tricia into a hug, the bowl pressing oddly between the two. She said gently, "Take this. It will always be yours."

Tricia held onto her aunt tightly as Aunt Mamie said in little gentle drops, "Keep on making snow cream. And rejoice. Don't ever forget."

This last profound lesson that Tricia taught me about affirmation is not to overlook life's yellow bowls. The yellow bowl is a symbol of our ability to accept and rejoice over whatever affirmations we receive, regardless of the source. Aunt Mamie was really telling Tricia, "You did the right thing. You brought joy. You gave. You loved. There is no greater success than this." Yes, there was pain. Yes, Tricia's mother never said the right words like, "I'm sorry, I love you." Nevertheless, Aunt Mamie did for Tricia what her mother now could never again do. Aunt Mamie acknowledged Tricia's faithfulness, her worthiness, and her triumph in the face of unforgivenness.

More often than not in our Waits, we form much too narrow a definition of the event that will satisfy us. Perhaps we have overlooked something as wonderful as miracle snow, the yellow bowl, and Aunt Mamie's benediction. Why not accept our affirmation from whatever source it comes, in whatever form it presently takes?

As we stare again into the highest injustice of the Wait with a sad signature on a last will and testament, oddly there is hope. Although Tricia never received the final pronouncement of her mother's love, she did receive the reassurance that she was a lovable person, worthy of love, a giver of love, and indeed loved. It was a simple yellow bowl, but it was a token of God's care, poured out through Tricia and to Tricia. As we peer into the empty bowl and see our faces reflected in wide, merry dimensions in the concave glass, we again hear Aunt Mamie whisper firmly, "Rejoice. It will always be yours."

Conclusion

During the Wait, we can accept the gift of affirmation from ourselves and from God. Our talents, hopes, and dreams were created by God, and he delights in us. How might we dare to put on life's sombrero today? How might we reach out and finally grasp the yellow bowl?

Taming the Envy Monster

5

Three of us were gathered around the lunch table: my husband Gordon, my sister Susan, and I. Gordon was chewing on a sandwich, and Susan and I were chewing up a book. Our juicy morsel was a small volume with the word *bridges* in the title that had been on the *N.Y. Times* best-seller list forever. It was billed as a transcendent love story. The plot was about an itinerant photographer and an unappreciated farm wife who finally found each other for one brief and shining moment. I did not detect any transcendent moments, but I did notice some detailed adultery.

I passed the book along to Susan telling her how dreadful it was. Susan was reading it at the table, and I was her audience of one, taking grim satisfaction in every roll of her eyes and every disgusted chortle. She read a passage out loud about the farm wife watching the photographer moving in his tight jeans, and I hooted, "Oh, please! This is pure elevated trash."

We must have gone on like this for fifteen or twenty minutes when Gordon finally deposited his plate by the sink and muttered, "Why are you two making such a big deal about that book? If it's that bad, why don't you just not read it?"

"You don't understand," I said defensively. "This thing's made the author world famous, and he's made bundles of money off of it."

"So?" Gordon asked.

"So, it's not fair. I've been writing for fifteen years about nice, decent things, and this guy hits the big time with something this awful, and they even made a movie of it."

Gordon just shrugged his shoulders, and I looked nervously back at the book. Why, indeed, had I spent twenty self-satisfying minutes ridiculing it? There was only one answer, and none of us said it out loud: jealousy.

While we may hold varying opinions on the particular bestseller under discussion at the lunch table, we do perhaps have at least one thing in common: a time or two we have all felt just a twinge of jealousy toward someone else who already has what we are so patiently awaiting.

Maybe seeing someone else's measure of success has caused us more than just a few pangs of discomfort. Perhaps it has cut us off from someone. Was it a co-worker who was promoted when we were passed over, or a neighbor whose marriage worked out finally when ours fell apart, or a friend whose child came back with her head on straight while our child was still in deep rebellion? Of course, we have been quite civil to them. Maybe we have even said all of the right things about how glad we are about their good fortune. But deep down inside, our stomach is wadded up, grumbling, "Why them and not me?"

In a previous chapter we spoke of hunger as an inescapable condition of the Wait, and in the same vein we must now turn to the issue of jealousy. Jealousy is quite like hunger in its omnipresence. We have not brought it on ourselves, nor will counting our other blessings make it go away.

Jealousy is also akin to hunger in our customary silence on the subject. One of the main reasons we do not talk about it is that it sounds so petty and childish. We are adults, and we feel we should be beyond jealousy. Yet if we examine the very adult ideas of business competition, constructive criticism, salary equity, poetic justice, performance ratings, status, love triangles, or sports rivalry, we understand that we never are through comparing ourselves with others, we never are through competing, and we never are through wanting what someone else has.

The other problem with jealousy is that it so often is disguised. During the lunch incident I was not aware that I was jealous. I felt that I was issuing a totally deserved and quite incisive literary critique. Jealousy can hide out as anything: stress, physical pain, chronic complaining, crusades, gossip, criticism, suspicion, ill humor, naysaying, depression, quarrels, or withdrawal.

The other thing that we need to make clear from the beginning is that getting rid of jealousy is not a hoop-jumping exercise. Cleaning up jealousy is not going to earn our long-awaited future. However, honestly dealing with jealousy will give us back the ability to enjoy oddly out-of-joint relationships in our lives. In addition, all of the mental energy that has been consumed by hiding, feeding, and excusing jealousy can be used on more positive and productive pursuits, like reaching on toward our future.

The Monster in the Dark

Since jealousy is sometimes so well camouflaged, we need to begin by fingering it precisely. The Latin root word for *jealousy* comes from zealous, connoting fervor or passion. One of Webster's definitions for jealousy is to be "hostile toward a rival or one believed to enjoy an advantage."

Although this nicely fits my lunch-table book critique, the waters are muddied when we glance at the other definitions of jealousy, which do not exactly apply to the Wait. These alternate definitions are all about what we already have, not about what we hope to get. They involve vigilance—sometimes healthy, sometimes not—in guarding and keeping a possession to ourselves. For instance, we might be jealous of a suitor who could steal the affections of our sweetheart.

Luckily another word gets right to the point of the Wait without dragging behind it any excess meaning: *envy*. Webster's dictionary says "envy" comes from a Latin root word meaning to "look askance" and "to see." *Envy* means "painful or resentful awareness of an advantage enjoyed by another joined with a desire to possess the same advantage."

This definition shook me up. The jealousy definition, the clause about "hostility" toward a rival, was my legal loophole. I could hide behind a cloak of self-righteousness by saying, "Well, I want what that person has, all right, but I'm certainly not being mean and belligerent toward him. It's nothing personal." But the definition of envy makes it apparent that we do not even necessarily have to harbor any sort of ill feelings toward the persons we envy, we just have to feel a stab of pain in our heart when we see them given what we so desperately want for ourselves. Finally, *envy* is a hard-working word, because it is both a noun and a verb. Envy is not just some state of mind that strangely happens to us like an outbreak of chicken pox. Envy also is something we actively do.

I was intrigued to discover that the King James Version of the Bible uses the word *envy* more squarely than my modern translation, which more often than not calls it jealousy. The first astounding fact that the KJV showed me was that we serve a jealous God, but not an envious one.

I had always puzzled over the Old Testament statements in Exodus, Deuteronomy, and Joshua where God is depicted as a jealous God (Exod. 20:5; Deut 6:14–15; Josh. 24:19 KJV). In light of our definition, I am beginning to see that it means that God has a passionate zeal about keeping us safely his.

His is a big love that does not want to see us go astray, a big love that would do anything to keep us in the fold, a big love that never wants to lose us to any lesser suitor.

On the other side of the fence is envy. The word *envy* is always applied to us mortals and never to God. This makes sense. What on earth (or heaven) could we possibly have that is not God's in the first place? Verses about envy are all over the KJV in the very places—Proverbs and the Epistles—that deal most practically with wise behavior among humans here on earth. Listen to the horrible company in a list of the worst of the worst that envy shares in the New Testament: evil, greed, vice, murder, deceit, malice, immoral and indecent actions, worship of idols, witchcraft, anger, ambition, drunkenness, orgies (Rom. 1:28–32; Gal. 5:19–21). Not only did envy make these hit lists, but it made the top ten, as in the "thou shalt not covet" (wish for enviously) in the Ten Commandments. It also made the early church's list of the seven deadly sins.

Apparently even angels can envy. Satan did (and does). After all, it was God's own throne he wanted for himself. And finally, and most chilling of all, envy was the underlying cause of the crucifixion of our Lord Jesus. The KJV states plainly, "For he [Pilate] knew that the chief priests had delivered him [Christ] for envy" (Mark 15:10).

Therefore, as we continue to talk about envy, we cannot just pretend that it is something minor and quite natural that goes bump in the dark like a loosely latched screen door. A real monster indeed is out there in the Wait, and he will get us quite surely if we do not soon turn on the light.

A Lesson from History

For a chilling picture of how envy can wreak havoc in the Wait, wander into the lives of a family in the Book of Genesis.

This is a two-generation story about envy between brothers and sisters. Jacob is born just seconds after his twin brother, Esau; they are constantly in cutthroat competition, even into adulthood. In fact, it becomes homicidal enough for Jacob to flee with nothing but a stolen blessing from their father, Isaac, and the robe on his back.

Jacob takes far off refuge with his uncle Laban, where the young man falls head over heels in love with Rachel, the younger daughter of Laban. Jacob has no wealth to pay for his bride, so he agrees to toil for seven years for Uncle Laban. Imagine Jacob's horror, when, after a wedding ceremony to a heavily veiled maiden, and an overnight honeymoon in a pitch-dark tent, he discovers he has really joined himself to Leah, the older and rather unattractive sister of Rachel! Uncle Laban gives a lame excuse about custom; the younger girl really should not marry before her older sister. After the seven-day wedding celebration, Jacob is allowed to take Rachel as his wife as well, but he must put in seven more years of indentured servitude to pay for her.

Jacob's unfortunate marital lot finds him torn between two sisters trying to share him as husband. Yes, the word *jealousy* applies aptly here, but it is the envy that ultimately plunges both sisters headfirst into the icy waters of the Wait.

On the surface Leah should be content. She has a husband; she is blessed with children; her physical needs are being met. But there is one elusive desire of her life that she cannot buy or earn at any cost. She longs with all of her heart for affirmation. Leah senses Jacob's great love for Rachel. It is painfully apparent, worth any personal sacrifice to him. If only Leah herself could be worth such utter devotion!

Maybe Leah accepts the fact that Jacob might never feel exactly that boundless joy about her. But, nevertheless, she hungers for the day when Jacob will not only say that he did not regret marrying her but that she is an important and valuable part of his life. Oh, to hear the words that she, too, has been worth every minute of seven years' toil! Listen to her longings as she names her first son Reuben, or "see, a son." "It is because the LORD has seen my misery. Surely my husband will love me now" (Gen. 29:32).

As we already have discovered, affirmation through event can be one of the most illusory tricks of the Wait. Leah bears a son for Jacob only to find that strangely it is not enough. She plays the mental game we have all played. She decides that if one son has not done it, then two surely will. She is terribly wrong. The second son receives the name Simeon: "Because the LORD heard that I am not loved, he gave me this one too" (Gen. 29:33).

We leave Leah still being crushed by the Wait, even though she bears son number three, Levi, and son number four, Judah. We tiptoe into Rachel's tent, and this, too, is not a happy place. Rachel is about to go out of her mind because there is one great desire of her heart that has not yet come true. Rachel is barren, and she envies Leah's motherhood.

"Oh, Rachel!" we want to cry out. "You are so loved! Count your blessings and be happy!"

Rachel answers back, "What good is such love? I'm a shame and a curse to my dear Jacob. He worked fourteen years out there with my father's herds just like a common slave. Think of the toil and the sweat! And now I can't even pay him back with a child!"

We want to tell Rachel that it is not her fault, but she cannot hear us because her culture brands her a failure. She finally lashes out in desperation to Jacob, "Give me children, or I'll die!" (Gen. 30:1).

Jacob answers, "What more can I do, Rachel? I'm not God."

At this point, the Wait has completely broken Rachel's wagon. Hunger drives her to try a quick fix. Rachel gives Jacob her slave girl. Sister Leah has gotten into a child-bearing slump after producing four sons, but she is not to be outsmarted by Rachel's scheme. Leah, too, gives Jacob her slave girl. What transpires is a sad litany of one-up-manship staged by the sisters using their poor maids as surrogates. They continue to claim the babies as their own, giving the maids' sons names like Naphtali, which sounds like "fight." Rachel gloats, "I have had a great struggle with my sister, and I have won" (Gen. 30:8).

Life in the Jacob household is far from a Norman Rockwell painting. The Bible gives us a graphic argument between the two sisters over mandrakes, a plant used as a love or fertility aid. Leah huffs, "Wasn't it enough that you took away my husband? Will you take my son's mandrakes too?" (Gen. 30:15). Rachel is so desperate for the mandrakes that she barters away a night in Jacob's tent in exchange for the plants.

How does the Wait finally turn out for these two women?

We never know if Leah receives Jacob's affirmation. Perhaps she finally does find some peace within herself. She names her sixth and final son Zebulun, which sounds like "accept" or "gift." "God has given me a fine gift," she declares. "This time my husband will treat me with great honor, because I have borne him six sons" (Gen. 30:20).

History records that Rachel does, in fact, receive what she wants. She bears two sons, but they are last in the family birth order, and she pays dearly for Benjamin when she dies in childbirth along the roadside to Ephrath.

At the end of the Wait, Jacob has twelve sons by four different women. The Wait may have ended, but it has left terrible scars on the entire family. The children, who have been used since infancy as pawns in this game of envy, are by now completely and utterly infected with the disease. The Bible says of Rachel's first son, Joseph, "When his brothers saw that their father loved him more than any of them, they hated him and could not speak a kind word to him" (Gen. 37:4).

Young Joseph adds his own vinegar to the sour stew by announcing quite indiscreetly, "I had a dream, and every one of you bowed down to me." This sends the brothers over the edge, and they conspire to murder Joseph. Only at the last minute do they impulsively sell him into slavery and report him as dead to their father Jacob.

As we get to the end of this sad story, we understand every one of the tragic characters. They are not horribly flawed people; they are people caught in a bad situation not of their own doing. They are all groping for faith, looking toward God for help, trying to live with elusive hopes, doing everything they can to reverse fortune and make it smile upon them. Finally, when they can fight fortune no longer, they give up and end up impotently fighting those who happen to be more fortunate.

It would be a powerful lesson for all of us if it ended here in the ashes, with a father continually mourning a beloved son, that same son bound into slavery, and the remaining sons guilty forever of a horrible crime and a colossal cover-up. We might close the book decisively, modulating sternly about the ugly monster in the dark, "And envy will get you if you don't watch out!"

The Turning Point

Luckily for all of us, the story goes on. Several decades later, something peculiar happens. A famine sweeps the land, and the ten brothers journey to Egypt to buy grain. Here the ten unknowingly fulfill the once-odious dream as they indeed bow down, unawares, to their brother Joseph.

Joseph knows exactly who they are, but the brothers do not suspect him of being anything other than an Egyptian ruler with the strangely thundering name Zaphenath Paneah, or "says the god: he will live." Joseph rather enjoys the ruse and goes to the length of addressing them through an interpreter, excusing his detailed nosiness about their family as an attempt to discover whether or not they are spies. The brothers have no idea that Joseph can understand every word as they mutter among themselves, "Surely we are being punished because of our brother. We saw how distressed he was when he pleaded with us for his life, but we would not listen" (Gen. 42:21).

We customarily cast Joseph as the hero of this whole saga, but there is another hero whom we seldom credit. While we temporarily excuse Joseph from the pedestal, he goes about constructing little cat-and-mouse games to test his brothers—accusations of spying, planting money in their saddle bags, false imprisonment, threats of slavery, not to mention the hostage taking of the most callous and blood-thirsty of the lot, Simeon, whose release can only be bought with Benjamin's arrival in Egypt.

In the meantime, our alternate hero, the unlikely Judah, journeys back home with the first caravan of grain. Nothing yet suggests that Judah, the fourth born of Leah, will someday distinguish himself. He is a person of wobbly conscience who presumably sat down to eat with the others while Joseph was hollering in the pit. Judah even came up with the idea of selling Joseph into slavery as sort of a macabre compromise: "Come, let's sell him to the Ishmaelites and not lay our hands on him; after all, he is our brother, our own flesh and blood" (Gen. 37:27).

When a second trip to Egypt must be undertaken for food, Benjamin is the sole means of buying Egyptian favor. An anguished family discussion takes place with their elderly father, Jacob. Perhaps because Judah has himself experienced the fatherly heartache of the death of two of his own sons, he is the one with enough passion to convince Jacob to allow Benjamin to travel to Egypt. Judah solemnly promises, "I myself will guarantee his safety; you can hold me personally responsible for him. If I do not bring him back to you and set him here before you, I will bear the blame before you all my life" (Gen. 43:9).

It is precisely here on the second journey back to Egypt that I envision the final transformation of Judah taking place. For the very first time Judah must become a true brother to Benjamin. Leah's son must at last become Rachel's son's "brother's keeper."

The Bible calls Benjamin a boy, although perhaps two decades have passed since Joseph was sold into slavery. Regardless of his age, we can guess that he has been spoiled into extended dependence, always the family baby no matter what his age. He never has been permitted to embark on a journey before, nor has he ever left his father for any period of time. Accordingly, we can hear Benjamin thrusting a thousand ill-conceived questions at Judah.

At first Judah goads his donkey, ready to leave this nuisance a few strides behind, but then he carefully reins back the poor, confused beast. Judah must remember to stay close to the youth. He must be Benjamin's protector, vigilant against marauders, beasts, and serpents. Judah has given his word. If an adder lurks in the path, Judah lets his own donkey balk and shoos away Benjamin's. On the afternoon rest, Judah makes sure that Benjamin has his share of the sparse provisions, even if it means eating and drinking less himself. The journey is lived around one simple principle: my life for Benjamin's life.

Judah starts out doing this for practical purposes: We'll all starve if we don't get more food from Egypt, and bothersome Benjamin is the price we're paying. But perhaps on the third night out, as Judah lies close to his youngest brother, the youth says with a faltering voice, "We've gone so terribly far, and Father is so old. What if we never see him alive again?"

Judah coughs away the thought and looks up into the immense night sky as Benjamin falls into a fitful slumber. Judah closes his eyes and pictures their father's face. The aged man's final wavering words creep into Judah's mind, "Yes, it will be my own death if something happens to Benjamin, but if I must lose my child, I will take this chance to save us all" (see Gen. 43:14).

Suddenly it all comes together for Judah. It is his father, not Judah, making the supreme sacrifice on this journey. Father is giving up Benjamin, the apple of his eye, so that they all might eat and survive! His father is, in effect, giving his life for them all. It is there, plain and unadorned yet full of the solemn splendor of piercing truth: "Father loves us all, and he always has . . ."

Judah's head is about to burst as he thinks, "How very odd! Only one thing has separated me from Father. It has been the comparing, the weighing, the dividing, the vigilance to see who gets what portion. But there is only one portion that matters. We are his sons, and Father cares for us. I will protect Benjamin because of Father's love."

This scene, of course, is conjecture. The historical account goes on to report that Judah does suddenly somehow find the courage to put his own life on the line to save Benjamin in the Egyptian courts. When Joseph trumps up a charge of thievery against Benjamin, Judah stoutheartedly steps closer to Joseph, making an impassioned plea based solely on his father's love for Benjamin, not knowing that this is the one argument that will indeed touch Joseph's heart to the very quick. Judah concludes, "Now then, please let your servant remain here as my lord's slave in place of the boy, and let the boy return with his brothers. How can I go back to my father if the boy is not with me? No! Do not let me see the misery that would come upon my father" (Gen. 44:33–34).

Joseph's head is pounding with emotion. His mind races, "Isn't this the fourth son of Leah, the one who sold me into slavery? How is it that he's now willing to become a slave himself to save Benjamin, the son of my mother Rachel?" Joseph dismisses his servants, for he is undone. He is no longer the in-control ruler, no longer a master chessman nor Zaphenath Paneah. He is again a boy in the pit begging for mercy that never comes. Great cries come out of him, and the years dissolve, "I . . . am . . . Joseph . . . your brother . . . whom you sold . . . into slavery."

His brothers are terrified. Their tongues are like stones. But great power has come into the room, power bigger and more important than any of them, eldest or youngest, most loved or most guilty. It is power beyond. It is God. Joseph proclaims, "And now, do not be distressed and do not be angry with yourselves for selling me here, because it was to save lives that God sent me ahead of you" (Gen. 45:5).

We would like to leave Egypt after this pivotal scene, which is not only the turning point of a family's story but truly the birth of an infant nation named Israel, now populated with brothers all.

Unfortunately, we cannot leave without one final warning. Envy has indeed been dealt a healthy blow, but partiality has not. Partiality will continue on through the ages and into our own modern-day Waits.

Joseph, in reckless joy over Benjamin, goes overboard by giving him three hundred pieces of silver and five changes of clothes. We cannot fault Joseph. He knew it was inequitable, but he already had given his other brothers much more than they deserved. Things are not always equitable in the Wait—thankfully. If things were fair, those ten half-brothers should have starved to death. It is no wonder then, that as the caravan readies to leave Egypt, we hear Joseph's last admonition ringing in our ears: "Don't quarrel on the way!" (Gen. 45:24).

Learning to Love Our Brother Benjamin

As we find ourselves back in the twenty-first century, we are heading on the journey of the Wait loaded down with various blessings and burdens. Joseph calls out after us, "Don't quarrel on the way!"

What he means is that to deal with envy we must learn to accept and love our brother Benjamin. We must set about it not necessarily because Benjamin is lovable but because he is our brother, and we both are loved by the same Father.

Loving Benjamin is not easy. Benjamin is the more favored one, the more protected one, the one with more gifts, the one held in higher esteem. These tangible gifts make him appear to be more favored than we are. Benjamin, being the youngest, was probably spoiled rotten and never had to take out the trash. He assuredly got a car for his sixteenth birthday and did not have to be in by eleven. Not only that, even as an adult the real Benjamin outdid everyone in the whole family by having ten sons.

How on earth can we be genuinely happy for Benjamin? How in heaven's name are we supposed to live out the admonition "Charity envieth not" (1 Cor. 13:4 KJV)? Through difficult experience, I have found that the best way to "envy not" the Benjamins in my life is to do as Judah did and journey a few miles down life's path with them. In the process of my really getting to know who they are and where they have been, they oddly become companions and not competitors.

At a writer's conference I once met a woman, ten years younger than I, whom I call Diane. Diane had enjoyed what I considered unprecedented success. She had completed only three stories and had all three accepted in a major magazine. I knew how hard I had struggled, the years and years I had gone from rejection to rejection. It did not seem fair. I had that suspicious, nagging, woozy feeling down in the pit of my stomach. I could call it something else, but it was, in fact, envy.

Diane and I talked for a bit, and more details of her life, other than the explosive success, began to emerge. She originally had been a secretary but always dreamed of writing. She made a gutsy decision to quit her job, move back with her elderly parents, and enroll in college to study writing. She was now doing full-time work writing ad copy for a pharmaceutical company, which sounded, quite frankly, deadly boring. She was happy to be earning a salary as a writer, but of course she would have preferred magazine work. As it was, any freelance story she wrote had to be snatched from a dead-tired mind. The particular article that had looked like such an effortless success had simmered in her mind for over a year before she was able to get it on paper.

You know, I think it was then that I stopped envying Diane and became her friend and encourager. I stopped comparing myself with her when I found out that she was as scared to death as I was of rejection. In fact, she had so little confidence in what I considered her promising talent that she was afraid to read the very magazines that contained her articles for fear her works would not measure up!

Here is what I learned from my experience with Diane. Most people we envy have indeed paid their dues in the Wait. We may not know it right away because we see them as one dimensional. We see only the one thing they have that we do not possess, not the many things we have that they do not.

Back to the real Benjamin. We complained about all of the things he had, the favors he got. We overlooked the one thing he never had. Benjamin never had a mother. It is a bit far-fetched to suppose that Leah or one of those slave women really and truly took the boy into their hearts. I am sure that Benjamin got fed, and somebody changed his diaper, but he never had a mother in that nurturing, you're-mine-and-I-love-you-just-because sense. Maybe, just maybe, that explains Jacob's fierce and unreasonable attachment to the boy; Jacob was trying to be both mother and father to Benjamin.

We have an objection simmering in the back of our minds. We have been thinking, "Well, perhaps we have misjudged a few Benjamins, but what if, once we get to know them, they turn out to be as bad as we thought they were? What if they got what they have by cheating or lying or stealing?"

This objection is quite valid. There are, in fact, cheaters, people who do not play by the rules, rogues who have no moral compunction, hustlers who did not pay their dues and do not ever plan to pay them. Proverbs has a practical dose of advice for us. Proverbs does not piously intone, "*If you're envious of evil people. . . .*" Not at all. The writer instead assumes that all thinking people will indeed be troubled by this inequity and will struggle to put it into some sort of reasonable context.

Proverbs 24:1 says, "Do not envy wicked men, do not desire their company." Proverbs 23:17–18 says, "Do not let your heart envy sinners, but always be zealous for the fear of the LORD. There is surely a hope for you, and your hope will not be cut off." Proverbs 24:19–20 says, "Do not fret because of evil men or be envious of the wicked, for the evil man has no future hope."

The harmonious strain in this trio of verses is the admonition not to let envy for the sinful be a concern of our lives. Yes, things are not fair, but since we cannot do anything about it, we should instead set our sights on our own positive future. Evildoers should be left to God. The Old Testament implications are that evil ones will not prosper forever, and therefore we should not "make friends" with their methods. There are such principles in the world as sowing and reaping, which eventually bring earthly consequences to bear on wrong choices. The evildoers may seem to have gotten away with something for now, but God will eventually deal with them, here or hereafter (see Ps. 37:1–2).

Faced with the deserving and the undeserving alike, we are left with only one viable option. Romans tells us plainly, "The commandments, 'Do not commit adultery,' 'Do not murder,' 'Do not steal,' 'Do not covet,' and whatever other commandment there may be, are summed up in this one rule: 'Love your neighbor as yourself'" (Rom. 13:9).

We return for one last visit with Jacob's family as the patriarch breathes an earthly farewell to each of his twelve sons. Jacob acknowledges his first three sons, but skips over them in favor of his fourth-born, Judah, to find a hand worthy of holding the royal scepter for generations to come (Gen. 49:10). Jacob pictures Judah as a lion, successful in the hunt, who goes and lies down in his lair. No one dares disturb his slumber, for he embodies a presence, even at rest, that creates untouchable awe and powerful respect.

Judah is strong because in mastering envy he has really mastered himself. He has been transformed by that pivotal moment when his own life finally mattered less to him than the life of his brother. Learning to love Benjamin changed Judah's life forever. Loving our Benjamins could do the same for us in our own slow wait for life's blessings.

Conclusion

As time goes on, partiality will continue, evildoers will cheat, and others 'round about us will appear to have more than they truly deserve. No wonder envy thrives and grows silently in the darkness of our hearts. We have been given only one true weapon against envy. This weapon is selfless love. Envy must flee in the face of such love as surely as darkness must flee from the light. Are we prepared to flip on the switch?

Laughter and the Fudgesicle
6
Waterfall

I grew up in the Washington, D.C., area, and on a sultry July day when I was ten years old, we took my visiting Minnesota grandmother and cousins downtown to tour the White House. To take the tour we had to wait in none other than the original killer line, the one that marked me for life.

This particular line was of the species lineus intermittious. This differs from its cousin, the lineus continuousa, where the line keeps moving like the ones at Disneyworld. In the lineus intermittious you stand still until your left hip hurts and the balls of your feet are pasted to your socks, and then suddenly everybody moves randomly forward anywhere from five baby steps to a hundred giant steps. This type of line is only surpassed in the production of stress toxins by the lineus rigor mortis, whose name requires no further explanation.

Along this same route were stationed sly, pushcart vendors who were betting on the fact that some misguided family of tourists would be foolish enough to try to survive this lineus intermittious with a ten-year-old girl in tow. Their bells sang like the sirens, offering fudgesicles for the ridiculous scalper's price of fifty cents in an era when milk was selling in the school lunchroom for two cents and a batch of those skinny newfangled McDonald's french fries was twelve cents.

I had to do a decent amount of nagging and sweaty hand tugging, punctuated with "pretty please with sugar on top." Finally, my parents agreed to let me leave the line, buy fudgesicles for all of the children, and then return.

I can hear my sandals flopping against the sidewalk as I skipped over to the vendor, awaited my turn, and at last purchased five fudgesicles. Then I turned. When I looked back I saw the lineus intermittious in sudden, mad motion.

When the lineus intermittious does move, it brings out the primeval predator instinct. As a space opens up in front, you pounce. When in fervent motion this line no longer has any individual members in it but instead consists of arms and legs filling up air pockets.

Trip, trip, trip went my sandals as I slowly went back to where I had left my family. No family. Trip, trip, trip up the line. No, they were not here, either. I stopped and considered. Maybe I was mixed up about where I had left them in the first place. Had it been by this tree or that tree? Again I roamed forward, then backward. My family was nowhere to be found.

A wiggle of worry worked through me, but I used the good head that had been put on my shoulders. Logic told me that my family was somewhere in this line. Therefore, they would eventually make it to the entrance gate to the White House. No problem; I would just wait for them there. This would have been an excellent strategy if the line had not been so long, the day so hot, and the fudgesicles so uncooperative.

There I stood next to a trash can at the black wrought-iron gate with those impatient fudgesicles. Actually they were not bad company at first, but it did not take long before I noticed this funny tickle that went across my wrist and down my arm all the way to my elbow. The same thing happened to the other arm.

Sometimes hindsight is twenty/twenty, and I wonder why I didn't think of three very logical solutions. Why didn't I pitch those fudgesicles into the trash on the first drip? And why indeed didn't I at least hold them down so they would drip on the ground and not on me? Better still, why on earth didn't I go ahead and eat those fudgesicles, one by one, until I had a royal stomachache? It might have prevented my becoming a chocoholic in later life. Instead, for some unfathomable reason, I stood there and let myself become a fudgesicle waterfall.

Now, fudgesicle waterfalls are rare natural occurrences, and people in the line seemed to stop discussing how Jackie Kennedy had redecorated the White House and started to take notice of this strange phenomenon standing at the gate.

I definitely was having no fun. About this time a lady waddled by in the line. She was wearing one of those sixties, oh-so-modern, horrible, orange, sleeveless shifts that made the wearer look like either a beached walrus or a tent pole. This woman was definitely of the walrus persuasion. When she rambled by, she noticed the fudgesicle waterfall. To replicate exactly how her statement sounded, you need to pinch your nostrils together and listen with someone else's ears. Here are her memorable words: "Deary, where on earth did you get those fudgesicles? Philadelphia?" Then she winked at me and was gone through the gate.

As you know, I survived into adulthood. My family eventually found me there at the gate. My dad pitched those melted fudgesicles into the trash where they belonged, and my grandmother used Kleenex and spit to clean up my sticky arms. They even let me in the White House, though I can probably lay claim to being the filthiest person ever to be admitted to the Blue Room.

The thing that surprises me about this whole story is that even after all of these years, I still recall vividly the precise words of the Walrus Lady. I remember them because they were funny, and they helped me get through a rather unpleasant time of being lost and waiting to be found. The Walrus Lady had nothing but humor to offer me. She could not locate my parents; she could not make the fudgesicles stop melting; she could not even give me her place in line. The only thing she could do was to offer me a cheery perspective, a kind of, "Oh my goodness, dear, isn't this the craziest thing that's ever happened to you?"

We are acutely aware by now that the Wait is serious business—futures and longings and hungers. But then again, Washington, D.C., is usually a very staid place until someone dumps a box of soap powder in the fountain in front of the Justice Department or a fudgesicle waterfall occurs. The sober and the quirky always mix in life, and when the two intersect, it is a relief and a gift. It is as if God frees us for a moment to laugh aloud and see outside ourselves, inside ourselves, and even around ourselves.

Humor seldom changes the actual situation, but it always changes our perception of it. Humor diminishes the terror and somehow reduces whatever we are facing to humble and manageable terms. *Laughter* has a fabulous root word. It originally meant to moo. When we rattle with laughter, we acknowledge the creatures we really are and that our pretenses of mastery and competence are, of course, quite amusing.

God and Laughter

The healing touch of laughter is indeed one of the graces that can help us through the long dreary hours, days, and months of the Wait. Even the stodgy and self-important field of modern medicine has embraced the benefits of laughter in recovery from illness. I recently read about a hospital that regularly sends a cart around the hospital floors; instead of magazines, it offers squirt guns and Groucho Marx disguises to the ill.

At first one might assume that the Bible is mostly silent on the matter of humor, since it is a book about the terribly solemn and serious subject of Almighty God trying to reach his hard-of-hearing people. This general feeling that frivolity is out of place is in one sense warranted. Perhaps that is why, as far as I can tell, a scarcity of verses directly addresses humor in the Bible. One of the few, Proverbs 15:13 (KJV), says, "A merry heart maketh a cheerful countenance." Although it makes a wonderful verse for framed calligraphy and cross-stitching, it seems to stand nearly uniquely alone in the larger sweep of the text.

Laughter itself is rarely mentioned in the Bible in the sense of good fun. In some cases laughter expresses derision—depicting evil persons scoffing or making fun of the righteous. On the other hand, the righteous laugh usually to express joy, relief, and celebration. Very little of it, however, is precisely mirthful.

Even the rare instance where a definite humorous laugh is attributed to a real person, we come away from the text with mixed signals. Sarah overhears two strangers telling Abraham that, at the ripe old age of ninety, she finally is about to get pregnant and bear a son. I can imagine Sarah's chin latching itself to her neck as she peers down at her robes and thinks about how everything on her body has gone south and not just for the winter. Who would not chuckle and shake her head at this absurdity? Just when we feel total kinship with Sarah, she wipes the grin off her face and mumbles to the questioning strangers, "Who, me laugh? Of course not. It must have been your imagination" (see Gen. 18:12).

If we look for a laugh track or punch lines in the Bible, we will be disappointed. That is not to say that there are no parts of the Bible that entertain us with incongruity and surprise. In otherwise serious stories, an imaginative reading or retelling can bring out the latent humor. When Balaam's donkey finally speaks back to him, he proves which two-legged character is indeed acting like a stubborn mule (Num. 22:22–35). And just think about the time the whale spits a wrinkled Jonah onto the beach like an unsavory hair ball. I can't imagine what his skin looked like after being basted in digestive juices for three days. And what about his hair? Maybe it turned green like modern hair does in chlorinated pool water. I guess I would repent, too, if a slimy prophet came to preach to me.

There is, however, one final biblical avenue of laughter to explore that customarily has been overlooked. Ecclesiastes 10:19 in the KJV tells us that "a feast is made for laughter." If feasting and laughter are inseparable, then good-humored laughter needs to be given very little direct mention in the Bible. We will hear laughter ringing in nearly every book of the Old and New Testaments when people sit down to feast.

Jesus himself is pictured as enjoying a good feast, not only on religious holidays but on other strictly social occasions, including a wedding and several dinner parties. This joyous feasting brought him his share of criticism from a procession of pious meddlers, criticism that Jesus soundly rejected. The type of age that Christ announced is more fit for exuberant feasting than long-faced fasting (see Luke 5:29–35).

Feasting starts out as God's idea when Moses gives it as an ever-hereafter commandment concerning the Passover. This national feast commandment is given even before the Ten Commandments spell out the moral code (Exod. 12:14–47; the Ten Commandments appear in Exod. 20). Later on, Moses adds two more national feasts that are connected with the two yearly harvests (Exod. 23:14–16). Most striking, this commandment is given to the very generation involved in one of the most grueling collective Waits ever recorded—the wilderness years during which the people await entry into the Promised Land. The commandment to feast comes at the very beginning of their ordeal, while the Israelites are still figuring that in a few weeks' time, they will be home and settled. God knows differently.

Although we may not celebrate these particular Old Testament feast days, they provide intriguing modern significance for the Wait. Ancient Israel is told to stop and make room for rejoicing and laughter at least three times a year. Feasting is a commandment, not an option. The nation is to feast obediently, regularly, regardless of current circumstances. It is their gift to God and God's gift to them.

Whether it has been a good year or a bad year, whether we have been waiting one year or thirty-nine, God invites us to the feast. He wants us to deliberately enter a season, a place, or a company where we can again laugh. Jesus himself feasts as recorded in the Gospel of John, despite circumstances that become more and more ominous and ultimately lead to his betrayal and death.

Not only can there be periodic times of feasting, but there also can be small feasts of laughter during any hour of life. Proverbs 15:15 (KJV) declares, "He that is of a merry heart hath a continual feast." Let us enter into the festivities.

Laughter amid Sorrow

In the beginning of this chapter, we mentioned the relief that laughter sometimes brings to not-so-funny situations, such as my girlhood experience of being lost. But does it also have a place in more serious undertakings, under the most dire of circumstances?

Barbara Thompson of Doraville, Georgia, was in such a situation. She had been called to California to her grandmother's bedside. From the age of four, Barbara had been raised by this plucky woman, and now Barbara was forced to spend long, agonizing hours in the hospital watching her grandmother waste into death.

Barbara's inner pain was unbearable. The hospital chaplain said, "We trust that God will show you a way to handle your pain." The next day the chaplain came around and asked, "Would you mind helping out another family? This young couple has a dying baby, and they need someone to watch their three-year-old for a few minutes so the parents can say good-bye to the baby together."

Barbara agreed. She was a mother herself and a school lunch room worker. She figured she could handle the job and that the break might offer a welcome change. Barbara left her vigil to take "Johnny" to the cafeteria for thirty minutes. The first thing the child did was race down the corridor, elbow his way into the elevator, and push every floor button. Out in the cafeteria courtyard, he knocked his milk squarely in Barbara's lap. The shock of the cold milk launched her out of the chair and had her practically doing jumping jacks as she slapped the napkin against the wet spot running down the legs of her beige pants.

The next thing that Barbara knew, Johnny had a landscaping rock in his hand, ready for a little target practice with the plate glass windows. Barbara sprinted over before he released the rock, grabbed Johnny by his shoulders, and squashed him back in his seat. Johnny took two bites of the hamburger and announced he had to go potty.

Everything went well in the ladies room until the flush died down and Johnny failed to unlock the stall. Barbara rattled the door and called his name. No reply. Barbara glanced under the partition. No feet. This was a very curious happening. Barbara assumed that the boy could not levitate, but she still was not quite sure how his feet had disappeared. As you know, there is only one surefire way to investigate what is going on in a locked stall in a public restroom. Barbara got down on her hands and knees and stuck her head under the partition.

What she saw inside was a little three-year-old boy straddling the commode, with one sneaker planted on each side of this watery and rather unorthodox pedestal. His hands were on his hips like a Power Ranger. Barbara is my age, and all she could think of was those old commercials of the Jolly—ho, ho, ho—Green Giant.

Something strange tickled inside of Barbara's throat, and there on the floor, with her soggy posterior pointed heavenward in a public restroom, she was overcome with laughter. This was no small, demure laugh; it was an overcoming laugh that had her slapping the floor with her hands.

Suddenly amid the commotion, Barbara heard a clicking sound: Johnny undoing the door lock. He had forgotten about his odd game and had come out to see what was wrong with this crazy lady.

Barbara gave Johnny back to his family and re-entered her grandmother's room, knowing that God had indeed shown her a way to handle the pain. She recalled that once as a girl her grandmother had been forced to place Barbara temporarily in a children's home. Her grandmother had wiped away a tear from the corner of her eye, straightened up, and said to the nun who was leading Barbara away, "Now, I want you to teach her to play the pie-ano." Barbara had gone away giggling instead of crying.

Barbara realized that laughter is a gift that can be used even in the midst of very serious and painful situations. Laughter can make the worst of Waits bearable. She pulled her chair up to her grandmother's bedside and whispered, "Let me tell you about a little boy I met today named Johnny."

As Barbara discovered, even when humor is inappropriate inside a sorrowful situation, the fresh breeze of humor will always be available outside. The amusement need not be large. It could be in watching a child trying to catch a puppy, or listening to two seven-year-old boys discussing girls, or it could even be in finding some strangely exotic food on the grocery store shelf.

One day when I was in a very bleak mood during the Wait, I came across a small can of pork brains in milk sauce at the grocery store. The can was tiny, just five ounces, and I got to wondering if the small can size represented the precise size of a pig's woeful cranial capacity or if it was instead calibrated according to the amount anybody can bear to eat at one time.

To some of us this might be seriously good eating, but it was the artist's illustration of the "serving suggestion" that invited me back to the continual feast. There was an outline of sky-blue plate and on it a bed of yellow globs; and on top of the yellow globs were little dollops of pink (the pork brains) that looked like migrating buffalo. My mother later enlightened me that the yellow stuff was meant to be scrambled eggs.

I bought those wonderful pig brains and put them in my cupboard. My children have nagged me from time to time to open the can, and I suppose I will on a day when I most need to be taken far beyond the Wait.

The Gift of Self-Laughter

Finally, because our situations are so serious during the Wait, we sometimes begin to take ourselves far too seriously. It is a wonderful gift to be able to throw back our heads and laugh about our own foibles. We will add a disclaimer. Good humor is always kind. It is inappropriate and unhealthy to constantly put ourselves down or to invite others to do the same. Self-deprecating humor sends mixed signals to everyone concerned. Therefore, self-laughter is healthy only when we feel quite grounded enough inside to share our amusement over something incongruent and common to humanity on the outside.

I learned a lesson in self-laughter quite well one summer as a chaperone on a teen mission-work camp. I like to carry on as much as the rest of them, but I am not too crazy about pranks. Unfortunately, on this last night of camp, the teenagers had a granddaddy of a prank planned for three in the morning.

I could not put the kibosh on this prank because there was an adult ringleader, a man who by day was a nice, conservative bank officer and chairman of our church finance committee. He sized up these interesting elements on the mountain hillside: the college-age camp counselors sleeping under a tin-roofed building sitting smack dab in the middle of a gravel parking lot. What would it sound like in the middle of the night to have rocks rain down over their heads? Why, it would sound like the Battle of the Bulge!

The teens gleefully added plans for an ambush of water balloons and shaving cream. There was even the detail of pulling the fuse out of the electrical box. Now, I believe in the old philosophy of live and let live, so I said nothing. Unfortunately, I got sucked into an unwelcome role in the caper when the girls in my cabin decided not to go to sleep, but to stay up until three.

Even that I could have withstood, except at two A.M. things got suspiciously quiet in the adirondack. No snickers, no whispers. I turned on my flashlight and caught the back of a girl right at the cabin opening, frozen like a deer in a car headlight. Every last girl had already sneaked out right past my bunk, and I had caught the very last one!

Of course I was not exactly Miss Congeniality at two in the morning, especially after six nights of sleeping on a piece of plywood. I got up, found the rest of the girls out by the outhouse, and gruffly ordered them back inside. I yelled at them, told them I was calling off the whole deal, and that I was going to get the counselors.

I did, in fact, huff down the dark mountain path with my teeny-weeny flashlight. A movement up ahead caught my eyes. I beamed my light to catch a lazy skunk waddling around on the path. I once owned a dog who encountered a skunk, and I had the pleasure of washing that dog down with a thirty-two-ounce can of tomato juice. I decided to reconsider my options.

I turned heel and headed back up another path, deciding that I would instead turn these girls over to Mr. Finance. Since it was his plan, he could baby-sit for the next pitch-black hour and have a close encounter with that skunk, thank you very much.

I got to the men's adirondack, and the fact that these fellows were slumbering so peacefully made me even madder. However, a new dilemma arose. Which one of those dark snoring forms was Mr. Finance? I finally made an approximate determination after taking my light around and sticking it in sleeping faces like an eye doctor. I leaned over the sleeping bag lump holding the rascal in question and began a scene that will long live in infamy. With my face hovering about six inches from his face and my right index finger wagging, I proceeded to awaken Mr. Finance from a deep and peaceful sleep by scolding, "All right Mis-ter Fi-nance. Get this thing over with and get it over with now!"

The poor man grabbed for his glasses and practically fell out of his bunk. Now really, at the time I was barely aware of the finger wagging. I did, after all, have a four-year-old at home, and I realized only later that the menacing index finger was my frequent "bad boy" warning. Whatever the case, Mr. Finance was now wide awake, and the fear of the Lord was in him. I left him writhing with this icy warning, "You're responsible now for these kids." Then I went back to my adirondack, told the girls to skedaddle, and lay down on my plywood to try to sleep.

It was blessedly quiet with all of those girls out of there. In fact, I might have even dozed off—until the noise came. I have never heard a rock slide or an avalanche, but this will serve me well enough for all future fiction-writing purposes.

Just imagine utter silence interrupted by twenty fistfuls of rocks heaved onto a sloping tin roof and then going thramba, ramba, knock-about-thunk as they slide off. It was indeed a masterpiece of mischief, a timpani of terror, a rafter-rattling ruckus worthy of a conniving white-collar banker going through the worst midlife crisis.

The sound was so startling and outlandish and utterly absurd, you know what happened? I laughed. It felt pretty good, but it also felt bad, because it kind of hurt my ribs when they jiggled against that plywood.

Well, the counselors took it as good sports, even the two fellows who fell victim to the water balloons when they ventured outside in the dark to confront their tormentors. Actually, that part fizzled in comparison to the mileage of laughter Mr. Finance got out of retelling about the finger wagging. Now that I have had some sleep, I guess it was all pretty funny after all.

I can laugh now because I learned something about myself. I wag my finger. I have accepted this strange fact about myself. I even have put some subsequent thought into my secret technique. This is what I do. I hold my index finger perfectly straight and then pop it at the wrist, like a woodpecker.

Conclusion

God's gift of humor can be ours, even in the midst of the longest of Waits. Although our situations may be quite serious, laughter can be a valuable escape valve. Humor can allow us briefly to step outside ourselves and our sorrow today. Welcome to the continual feast. Why not moo out loud?

Planting Apple Trees

7

in Babylon

Once I spent three days in a men's restroom. This particular restroom was a seven-by-ten space in an old decommissioned elementary school. On the left-hand cinder block wall were two small, mineral-stained sinks. On the end opposite the door were some cracked, frosted windows, and on the right was a urinal and one toilet without a stall around it. It was not the type of place that invited a stay of more than five minutes, much less a stay of a long weekend as I was planning along with four other women.

We had not lost our minds nor were we being held hostage. The men's restroom was simply the only space available for a round-the-clock prayer vigil on our women's retreat. Before we got to praying, we got out the Comet. We scrubbed everything up and then we covered it up. We put a board across the two sinks for a shelf and threw a tablecloth over it. On the shelf went baskets, note cards, Bibles, potpourri, and peppermints.

More fabric and masking tape covered the commode and the urinal. We brought in an area rug and cushions. We put up posters, and in the corner we propped a seven-foot banner with a cross and crown on it made in luxurious purple satin with gold fringe. We plugged in a tape recorder, put on soft praise music, and lit scented candles. The room was admittedly small and a bit awkward because of the covered-up commode, but the air conditioning in there on that hot May weekend was superb. Air conditioning always seems to be intense in restrooms, whether or not you want it to be.

The following day a woman from the kitchen crew stepped in to deliver a frantic prayer request about the rolls not rising and the oven acting up. As she stood there, her shoulders began to loosen, and her face relaxed. She wiped the sweat off her forehead and lingered several moments, sighing. "This place is so peaceful and pleasant. What a wonderful place this is!" We smiled. Obviously, she had not seen the room when it was all urinal and sink.

During the Wait we often are forced to occupy strange and unlikely places quite against our will. We must make do the best we can, turning sinks into shelves and pretending that commodes are anything but commodes. It might be a geographical location like a job, a house, a neighborhood, a church, a school, or a region that we would rather leave behind. On the other hand, it might not be a physical place, but rather a situation that we would much rather escape—a relationship, a marriage, a financial burden, a disease, a disability, an emotional problem, an overwhelming responsibility.

Whatever the case, we are, quite bluntly, trapped. While we await our hoped-for life change, this is, unfortunately, our home sweet home, and it will take more than the hasty redecorating job we did on the men's room to make it pleasant and bearable. Our chapter on affirmation dealt with enjoying *who* we are as we wait, and this chapter is about being comfortable *where* we are as we wait. How can our faith make our in-the-meantime lives in inhospitable spots more livable, likeable, and even productive?

Jeremiah's Advice about Life on Hold

Exactly one person in all of Jerusalem and Judah can stomach Jeremiah—Baruch, his scribe. No one else likes Jeremiah, because he is unerringly fatalistic. If someone remarks about the cool, northern breeze, Jeremiah replies, "From the north disaster will be poured out on all who live in the land" (Jer. 1:14). If someone crows, "Great news! My sister's getting married next week," Jeremiah shakes his head sternly and laments, "My abject condolences. She will only have children who will starve to death, and their bodies will rot in the streets." In short, he is a man set apart by God's burden, unfit for society, labeled a madman who deserves to be chained in an iron collar.

Not only is Jeremiah charged with the thankless job of being the national broadcasting system of doom, but even worse, his own personal life is put on indefinite hold. God commands, "'You must not marry and have sons or daughters in this place.' For this is what the Lord says about the sons and daughters born in this land and about the women who are their mothers and the men who are their fathers: 'They will die of deadly diseases. They will not be mourned or buried'" (Jer. 16:2–4). God further instructs Jeremiah not to feast and not to mourn, not to laugh and not to cry. Jeremiah not only is amputated from society, but he becomes a tortured man cut off from his own mortal body and his own natural emotions.

No wonder Jeremiah rails, "Whenever I speak, I cry out proclaiming violence and destruction. So the word of the Lord has brought me insult and reproach all day long. But if I say, 'I will not mention him or speak any more in his name' his word is in my heart like a fire. . . . I am weary of holding it in; indeed, I cannot. Cursed be the day I was born!" (Jer. 20:8, 9, 14).

This unhappy drama goes on, year after year, through the reign of one king after another, one message of privation and damnation after another. Finally, after Jeremiah has been preaching like a broken record for more than twenty years, his predictions come true. King Jehoiachin surrenders Jerusalem, and the ruling class is taken off into Babylonian captivity.

Jeremiah does not let up but preaches an even more inflammatory message to those remaining in occupied Jerusalem: submit to the captors, abandon plans for an armed rebellion, cooperate with the enemy, wait for God to act. Just when it seems his messages cannot possibly become any more diametrically opposed to mainstream opinion, Jeremiah dictates a letter to the Babylonian exiles. What a startling letter it is! Here is what he writes:

> Build ye houses, and dwell in them; and plant gardens, and eat the fruit of them; Take ye wives, and beget sons and daughters; and take wives for your sons, and give your daughters to husbands, that they may bear sons and daughters; that ye may be increased there, and not diminished. And seek the peace of the city whither I have caused you to be carried away captives, and pray unto the LORD for it; for in the peace thereof shall ye have peace (Jer. 29:5–7 KJV).

This letter leaves us gasping. The tortured man who never allowed himself any sort of a life is suddenly telling the captives to do in Babylon what he has never permitted himself to do in the homeland of Jerusalem. He tells them to embrace life in their foreign land, to put down roots, to build, to dwell, to marry, and to have children. Not only that, they are actively to work and pray for the enemy city! Perhaps there finally are forbidden personal tears in the crusty prophet's eyes as he admonishes them not to put off life one

minute longer but to put life back on, despite the hostile sur-
roundings.

The Jewish leaders are completely outraged. They counter,
"There can be no good life in captivity. Ever! Certainly it will
only be a year or two before we're restored, not the seventy
years Jeremiah predicts. Don't listen to him. Never compromise. Make yourself angry and anxious and motivated to get
out at all costs. Expect liberation. Demand it of Yahweh. Shake
your fist skyward! Don't put down even the tiniest of roots.
This isn't your home and never will be. Loathe it with all of
your hearts, loathe the city, loathe the rulers, loathe the oppressors, loathe the very ground. Abide peacefully never."

Behind their ranting is dogmatic, religious zeal. There is
a bigger, uglier reason that they think the exiles must not
stay: Babylon is a heathen nation, and God would not think
of dwelling there. God lives only in Jerusalem among the
chosen ones. The religious leaders spit on the ground when
they hear that Jeremiah has said to pray for Babylon. They
smugly mutter among themselves that God has little chance
of hearing such prayers anyway, for "they are far away from
the LORD" (Ezek. 11:15).

The exiles are torn in half. Fight or settle, rebel or build?
When they meditate on what the religious leaders have said,
they despair. "We shall surely all die anyway now if Yahweh's
reach doesn't extend into this foreign place. Why not at least
fight it then? We're already cursed and thrown onto the scrap
heap of life, sentenced to a living grave. Once we lived in
God's shadow, but now we live in the pit of hell."

As this anguish trickles down their forsaken cheeks, God
stirs a mighty wind along the banks of the Chebar River in
Babylon, sweeping aside time and space to visit Ezekiel, one
of the exiles, with an unparalleled vision of a heaven full of
unspeakable beings of light and power. This vision comes
not to the high priest in Jerusalem, not to the ones who
boasted of still possessing the Promised Land as the mark
of God's approval, but to Ezekiel, a captive in Babylon.

Ezekiel emerges from the vision boldly proclaiming God's message: "Although I have cast them far off among the heathen, and although I have scattered them among the countries, yet will I be to them as a little sanctuary in the countries where they shall come" (Ezek. 11:16 KJV). God has broken in, and finally Jeremiah's advice makes complete and utter sense to the captives. God is here, even in Babylon. Because he is here, we can somehow indeed abide peacefully and prosper after all.

We, of course, are exiles of the Wait. God has put within us a longing for a true home that is not yet ours. In the meantime we can live, because he promises to be for us a "little sanctuary" in our foreign home. His sure advice to us today is that issued from the pen of Jeremiah's scribe centuries ago, "Plant apple trees in Babylon."

Jeremiah's letter is not about temporary wayfaring. It is instead about long-term living. The KJV uses the word *fruit* to describe the planted gardens. Fruit is not something that grows in just one short season like lettuce. A fruit tree takes a number of years before it is large enough to bear. Even after that, according to Levitical law, Israel was to consider the fruit ritually unclean for three years, then to dedicate the fruit entirely to God in the fourth year. Finally, in the fifth year, they were to eat the initial harvest (Lev. 19:23–25).

There is no reason for those expecting a short, two-year stay to plant an apple tree in Babylon. Why do such an act when they never would receive the benefits? Worse still, they would leave behind something good for their undeserving captors. And yet God says quite ridiculously, "Plant apple trees in Babylon."

Today there are other reasons we hesitate to plant apple trees during the Wait. I doubt if any of us is worried so much that someone less deserving will benefit unfairly from our abandoned toil. The truth is, we have listened to the badgering false prophets who, in the name of religion, tell us that it would somehow be disloyal to our dreams to get on with life as we find it today. Should not we fight with all of our might against the life that is, because it has precluded the life that once was or is yet to come? Jeremiah shakes his head and forms a silent no. He tells us that the answer is not in fighting but rather in abiding in simple, life-affirming trust. For now, this unlikely waiting room is our God-given home.

The Concept of Abiding

Abide is an old-fashioned word seldom used these days. I recall seeing it on a sign only once. We were living in Charleston, South Carolina, and a garden center out on Mount Pleasant was named "Abide-a-While Nursery." The garden center was situated under the cool spreading shade of live oaks, and it was full of fresh, lush, well-watered azaleas, camellias, and holly ferns in black plastic pots. The spot lived up to its name. I wandered the good part of an hour, enjoying the braggadocio faces of rose-and-white striped camellia blossoms.

The word *abide* means to await, but its derivation is the same as *abode,* which means home or a place of sojourn. Abiding in this sense means dwelling, residing, or sojourning. Perhaps it is good fortune that the word today has so little cultural meaning for us, for it remains fraught with the splendor and power of the language of the King James Version of the Bible. Recall this verse: "He that dwelleth in the secret place of the Most High shall abide under the shadow of the Almighty" (Ps. 91:1). The words *dwell* and *abide* bring many wonderful feelings to this verse: relief, safety, covering, protection, rest, communion, welcome.

Even more splendidly, the word *abide* is the hinge in the KJV on which one of the loveliest of all verses moves: "Abide in me, and I in you. As the branch cannot bear fruit of itself, except it abide in the vine; no more can ye, except ye abide in me" (John 15:4). Suddenly the word *abide* connects electricity into our veins. Something flows through us that has its very source in God. It is kinetic and organic, bringing forth fruit from dryness. We no longer exist in a suspended, incomplete state. We are planted, rooted, growing, blooming, and bearing fruit.

To abide suggests the hospitality, presence, and protection of a host. God himself is our host, a "little sanctuary" away from the permanent one. Abiding implies sustenance, connection, and firm, constant help. Therefore, during the Wait, we are not called on merely to endure a parched, shrunken version of life but rather to be conduits of life. Our lives are fruitful, even in a hostile environment.

Unfortunately, we definitely can choose not to abide. We do not even have to ferociously fight against where we are; we can simply neglect to do any real living. I once spoke with a man who had made a decision not to abide in his marriage, and he did not even know it. His wife had been unfaithful to him several years earlier; the affair had ended; and the couple had remained married. On the outside they looked like a normal, busy couple, but on the inside, things were quite barren and nothing was growing. The man was living in limbo land, strangely not at home in his own household. He still held onto divorce as a trump card, and he was waiting it out to see if his wife would stray again. If she did, that was it. So there he was, married, but unwilling to invest any emotional energy, affection, or love in his wife lest it later turn out to be a dead-end venture.

What if this man took Jeremiah's advice and went ahead and again lived in his marriage as if he would be in it forever? What if he decided to plant apple trees? He would take the time to find something—anything—to build on. He would let go of his fears, his reservations, and his vivid, nagging images of what once was, and he would nourish the wounded but still-lingering love inside his heart. He could "pray unto the LORD" for his wife and "seek the peace" so that "for in the peace thereof shall ye have peace" (Jer. 29:7 KJV). The man would then dwell in a new and unusual place of trust. He would then be trusting not his errant wife but the host with whom he was abiding—the Heavenly Father. The man would live more prosperously and more fully, despite the less-than-ideal situation and the continuing uncertainty of tomorrow.

Before we go on, we shall add that common sense dictates that there are, indeed, places too dangerous to abide. There will be exceptional cases where God directs us to withdraw at all costs. For instance, we would be ill-advised to stay in a situation where we or our children are subject to abuse, deprivation, or mental harm. Competent outside help should be used to help us determine when the situation has crossed over the line. Beyond this, however, God's general rule for us in the Wait is to abide where we are. It is not a sentence. It is instead a gracious invitation.

A Modern-Day Trip to Babylon

The first and foremost thing you notice about Peggy Michaels of Chattanooga, Tennessee, is her smile. Her smile is not small and faint; it radiates across her face and pulls up her ears and chin and crinkles her dancing eyes. Peggy grew up in a family that always looked on the bright side of life. Her growing-up years were full of praise, encouragement, and success. She was given plenty of natural reasons to smile.

But these days Peggy's smile is supernatural. After all, she has been sent to live in Babylon three times. Of course, Peggy does not call her misfortunes "going to Babylon." She calls them "bumping a bad place in life."

Peggy's first trip to Babylon was geographical and financial. Her husband's business folded, and they were forced to sell their home and take their two young daughters to Florida to start over again. The second time around, Peggy's life was under siege on another front; her marriage fell apart. Peggy fought against divorce with everything she had, but she was eventually forced into the exile of single motherhood, raising and supporting her children through her work as a physical education teacher.

And then came the third and most distressing trip into captivity.

It all started out as a vague numbness in Peggy's feet. This symptom was strange for someone who loved tennis and water skiing and who had beaten all of the boys in foot races in elementary school. First she gave up tennis because she started having difficulty with side-to-side movement. Then she gave up water skiing because her balance was failing her. She went to a doctor, and he gave her a shocking diagnosis: possible multiple sclerosis.

Peggy left the doctor's office thinking, "No, it's not possible. I've been so active all of my life." Peggy tried to stay positive and upbeat, throwing all of her mental powers into ignoring everything but wellness.

Peggy took on a demanding schedule teaching physical education at three elementary schools where she soon developed an outstanding program that emphasized individual improvement and not competition. Peggy decided not to put awkward six-year-olds at the plate with no chance of hitting the ball. Instead, she kept something in each student's hands all of the time: rhythm sticks or colorful light-as-air juggling scarves. The children learned body parts and coordination by hitting balloons on elbows, knees, and ears. They swatted homemade yarn balls with a paddle fashioned from coat hangers and stretched hosiery.

The headmaster at Girls Preparatory School, a local private high school, heard about Peggy's work and offered her the dream job of physical education department head. There she was able to develop a completely new curriculum designed to promote lifelong fitness habits for teenage girls. It seemed that her life was at last back on track. She was finally back home.

Peggy had been on her new job only a few months when she was walking brisk laps with the girls in the gym. After they had done about a mile, Peggy heard a strange cadence: thump-thump, scwrunch. The "thump-thump" was the heel and toe of her right foot quite normally slapping against the floor, and the strange "scwrunch" was her unresponsive left foot being weakly dragged forward. Peggy shrugged it off with a nervous smile.

G. P. S. sits on a bluff overlooking the river, and a lower athletic field sits on the riverbank, accessible from the school by a daunting flight of stairs down the cliff. Peggy eventually had to swallow her pride and drive her car down the bluff to the lower field because her stamina was indeed failing. What made it all the more embarrassing was that she had driven down to administer timed fitness runs.

In January of 1990 her doctor confirmed what Peggy's body had been slowly telling her all along: multiple sclerosis. Unfortunately, the diagnosis was the only definite news. There was no known cause, no known cure, and no way to predict how quickly it would progress or what muscles it might affect next.

Peggy was being taken the worst prisoner of all. She was the prisoner of her own body. She was being forced away on her final trip to Babylon, and she was helpless. She crept back into her small condo and dragged herself up to her loft bedroom thinking, "Eventually I won't even be able to make it up these stairs."

Peggy fell on her knees by her bed and cried out to God, "Lord, I can't do it. This disease is going to take everything away from me. I can't be a financial provider. How can I be a PE teacher with MS? And how can I be a good parent to my girls and not a burden to them? And who'll fix the car when it acts up? I thought you promised you wouldn't give me more than I can handle." No answer came to Peggy. She got up knowing only one thing. She knew that she was helpless and that God would have to take care of it all somehow.

Peggy began searching again for spiritual support, something that she had in the past, but had not re-established since her divorce. She found a Sunday school class and asked for prayer. Her request? For release so that she could continue to let God into her life.

Peggy found two books that helped her immensely, one that recommended that she saturate herself in God's Word. As she did, her faith grew, and she could hardly wait for her nightly devotional time. Through a year of study, one thought sat in Peggy's mind that felt like a personal promise: "I won't get well right away. God is going to heal me from the inside out."

God did not relieve Peggy of her physical symptoms, but as promised, he did begin to relieve her of her worries. One of Peggy's worst fears was of being a burden and an embarrassment to her teenage daughters. One spring day, through a small incident, God reassured Peggy that even her younger daughter, Kingsley, could handle Peggy's disability with grace and maturity.

That Saturday Kingsley expected a ride to the Walnut Street bridge where she hoped to see her prom date cross the finish line in a rowing regatta. But at the last minute the ride fell through. Peggy jumped into the car with Kingsley, but when they arrived on the riverfront, there was nowhere to park. After parking countless blocks away, the two set out at a fast pace trying to make it in time. Soon Peggy began to tire, but she was much more concerned about Kingsley's disappointment if they arrived too late. Peggy suggested with false bravado, "Sweetheart, why don't you just run on, and I'll catch up with you in a minute?"

Kingsley stopped and answered, "Mom, It's O.K. We're not in that big of a hurry. You just lean on me."

Peggy was touched and grateful that Kingsley would quietly set aside her own teenage do-or-die determination about seeing the race to help her mother. Peggy placed her hand on Kingsley's young shoulder, and it gave her enough balance and confidence to walk briskly onto the bridge. The two arrived in time after all—together.

As the two cheered the finish of the race, Peggy thought, "All of these years I've been walking with Jesus, but I've never really leaned on him." In accepting the offer of that simple handhold on the steadying shoulder, Peggy had stopped fighting against the restraints of dependence. She was ready to accept it as part of the strange new territory in Babylon.

That fall Peggy got up enough boldness to ask for prayers of healing. If this were a book about any other subject but the Wait, we might expect that the story had been recounted so that we might wipe away a tear or two of joy at the happily-ever-after ending of a physical healing. The ending is quite different. Peggy explains, "My physical healing did not take place at that time, but since then I have let go of so much anger and anxiety. I have a peace about where I am."

Although Peggy had always been an upbeat person, life sometimes holds terrible downbeats. She was brought, just like the Babylonian captives, from a false human optimism about quick delivery into a place of abiding trust in God. She learned that sometimes the most faithful lives are ones lived to the fullest, despite exile and captivity.

Peggy was ready to plant apple trees. One day she planted six hundred when she gave a talk to the six hundred students at G. P. S. She aptly entitled her speech "A Celebration Out of Adversity." Many of the girls did not know that Peggy had multiple sclerosis. In her talk Peggy explained about the disease and told about her denial and the help that had come when she acknowledged her problem. She concluded, "Even though I don't water ski anymore, I can still drive the boat. I may not be playing volleyball anymore, but I can still coach. I serve every serve my players serve and win and lose with them every game they play. . . . I may not run a race anymore, but I can be at the finish line to congratulate you."

The assembly was hushed. Afterward hundreds of girls used their lunch hour to stand in line just for the opportunity to hug Peggy as they went out the door. Notes and letters poured in. Girls stopped by her office to thank her and to talk over their own times of adversity. The apple trees were growing.

Another type of apple tree Peggy began planting freely was thankfulness. Instead of lamenting her need for the school elevator, Peggy thanked God that it had been put in just when she had begun to need it. And the drive down to the lower field was now helpful, not embarrassing. She could still pitch a Wiffle ball with the seventh grade girls. She just "borrowed" the young legs of two girls who could chase after the ball for her and toss it over, so she could pitch again.

The most unusual twist of all came when Peggy was voted the Tennessee Secondary Physical Education Teacher of the Year for 1993–94 by the Tennessee Association for Health, Physical Education, Recreation and Dance. The committee knew only of Peggy's work, and nothing of her illness.

Peggy awaits physical healing. At this writing, it has not happened yet, although she remains hopeful of new medical breakthroughs perhaps on the horizon. She is involved like all of us in the Wait, and this period of exile goes with the territory. Nevertheless, Peggy continues to smile. Like all of us, she has her good days and her bad days, which makes her smile all the more precious indeed. Smiling is possible because Peggy has learned to abide. And in the meantime, she has an abundant harvest of well-cultivated fruit to sustain her.

Conclusion

During the Wait, we are forced to live in strange and hostile spots. God invites us to stop fighting the circumstances and instead to go on and live life to the fullest, right here, as we await his deliverance. In fact, God has given us an assignment in the meantime. He wants us to make a few lasting home improvements. How many different varieties of apple trees can we plant?

Prayer and Hearing from God

8

As I was researching this book, I visited the local Christian bookstore and asked where I might find a book on waiting. The perplexed clerk told me that he carried no such title, though there was probably something on the microfilm catalogue I could order.

"Surely in one of these books in here there's something on the subject of waiting," I prodded.

A small smile finally passed across the clerk's face as it dawned on him where I most likely could find something about unfulfilled longings. He pulled me over to the Christian Living section and said brightly, "Here. There's bound to be something in these books on prayer."

Prayer? I stood in stunned silence. Without knowing it, the clerk had dished out a shocking truth. Waiting is not only the black eye of life, but it is, quite frankly, the black eye of prayer as well.

During the Wait, we are the persistently knocking neighbor in Luke 11 who practically tears down his neighbor's door in the middle of the night in search of bread. Jesus says, "I tell you, though he will not get up and give him the bread because he is his friend, yet because of the man's boldness he will get up and give him as much as he needs" (Luke 11:8).

This is the troubling story of our prayer lives during the Wait. We have been asking. And asking. And asking. Forever. Our knuckles are raw from beating on the door. Our throats are hoarse from calling out. We might even be called bold, if boldness means shamelessly and persistently uttering the same request over and over again. There is only one problem with this parable from Luke. Our life situations are still on hold. No one has yet opened the door to finally give us what we so ardently want and need.

Because of this, confusion settles over our prayer lives just when we desperately need to hang onto prayer as a lifeline. How on earth can we keep our prayer lives healthy given the slow water torture of the Wait? Prayer is a far-reaching subject, and, of necessity, this chapter deals with it in basic terms of communication. During the Wait we need assurance that God has heard us, and we need to hear back from him concerning daily guidance that might well affect our future.

Has God Heard?

Peek into a five-year-old child's room at bedtime and listen to her nightly prayers. "And bless Mommy and Daddy and Doggie. And please, God, make it snow tomorrow. Amen."

We might not cringe during January in Buffalo, New York, but we might if we live in Atlanta, Georgia. As rational adults we know that it may not snow tomorrow. When a clear, crisp, snowless morning dawns, the efficacy of the child's spontaneous and believing prayer is going to be called into solemn question. It will seem as if God has not heard.

Interestingly enough, such a frustration in prayer is not a reflection of faith but rather a reflection of culture. The underlying problem is not God but science. Our society idolizes scientific reason based on cause and effect. The outcome and effectiveness of any endeavor, big or small, is judged by concrete, measurable, short-term results. No wonder we are tempted to frame the effectiveness of prayer in these terms: Did we promptly receive what we requested? Unfortunately, during the slow-going Wait, the answer is unerringly and continually a resounding no.

The time restraints are not the only stickler when trying to apply scientific procedure to prayer. Since we have been taught that all equations must balance, it is no wonder we wrongly assume that not only must the providential event quickly follow our prayers, but that the answer must also match up with the careful wording of our original requests.

Thankfully, prayer does not work this way. As an example, perhaps the five-year-old girl who prayed for snow was, without being aware of it, actually feeling, "I need something wonderful and fun to break into my dull life soon." Now, snow might have been nice, but it would in short measure melt and be gone. Instead, the young girl might trot off to kindergarten on that next snowless morning and meet a new girl who will turn out to be her very best friend for the rest of her life.

The ancient hearers of Jesus had no such difficulty with Luke 11 when he says, "Which of you fathers, if your son asks for a fish, will give him a snake instead?" (Luke 11:11). They did not view it as a mathematical formula that means asking for a fish equals getting a fish. Instead they understood that the father in question knows instinctively how to give good things. No father would give something harmful and inedible to a child who is hungry; neither would God.

Leaving our culture and rejoining the Kingdom brings new freedom into our prayer lives. We understand that God does not require any sort of precision in our prayers, he simply honors the fact that we *are* praying. He hears not only the words, but also the spirit of the prayer in the context of his loving desire for our welfare. Paul assures us, "In the same way, the Spirit helps us in our weakness. We do not know what we ought to pray for, but the Spirit himself intercedes for us with groans that words cannot express. And he who searches our hearts knows the mind of the Spirit, because the Spirit intercedes for the saints in accordance with God's will" (Rom. 8:26–27).

My sister Susan was experiencing the frustration of unanswered prayer when we attended a church service together. Susan's husband had been on a two-year job search following a lay-off. She described the chronic stress, "Sometimes it feels like we're slowly drowning. What if the car breaks down, or I get sick or we get too far behind in the rent? I'm worried about going under one final time."

We stood to hear Luke 11 read as the lectionary passage. When it came to the part about the persistently knocking neighbor, Susan leaned over and whispered to me, "Yeah, that's me. I've been knocking. Only problem is, nothing's happened!"

Susan's whispered dilemma was still fresh on our minds as we settled into our seats for the sermon. The minister, Reverend Mark Sargent, read the parallel verse in Matthew that says simply that God will give us "good things." Then he re-read Luke 11:13, "If you then, though you are evil, know how to give good gifts to your children, how much more will your Father in heaven give the Holy Spirit to those who ask him!"

Susan's mouth fell open; so did mine. On the other side of the door is not some fleeting piece of consumer goods, not simply some temporary "good thing" that might relieve today's stress without provision for tomorrow's. No indeed. On the other side of the door is God himself! The astonishing result of prayer is that God, the Comforter, comes to dwell with us.

The bedrock problem with our results mentality was that we were looking for too small and temporary a result. God turns the tables on the knocking parable by saying, "Listen! Here I am! I stand at the door and knock: If anyone hears my voice and opens the door, I will come in and eat with him, and he with me" (Rev. 3:20). The question, then, is not whether or not God has heard. The true question is whether or not we have heard.

Hearing from God

I once attended a writers' workshop where we had to read each person's piece and say where we thought readers might question its verisimilitude. *Verisimilitude* means something that has the appearance or sound of the truth. Not only did the writing have to be true, but it also had to sound and feel true against the backdrop of the reader's personal and practical experience.

In one manuscript a writer recounted how God had given her very specific instructions for presenting a gift to a stranger. The instructions said exactly what to give, where to find it, and even included specific comforting words of faith to say while she handed this gift to the stranger. In the story, the writer went so far as to put the instructions in quotation marks, as if the directions were part of a real conversation. A lively discussion ensued among the writers. Was it stretching credulity to portray God speaking to individuals with such clear words in ordinary, suburban kitchens that one might even dare put quotation marks around it?

There was no consensus among the writers that day, and I left the conference still mulling over the matter. If it were true that God could speak so specifically to individuals, why were there so many of us who did not seem to hear? And if he did speak, why not just tell us how our Waits would end so we could get on with life?

Soon after, I met a woman I call Millie. Millie was in her midforties; she had just met Jesus, and she was still beaming like a lighted neon sign. Millie knew that I was a writer, so she phoned me one day saying, "Would you come over? I want to share with you what the Lord has been doing in my life."

I obediently arrived with my tape recorder, pressed the record button, and listened to Millie's breathless description of new and quite specific directions and revelations that came to her daily, even hourly. Finally, I asked Millie point blank, "How do you know that it's God telling you these things?"

She answered bluntly, "So far I've told you all of the good things. Some of the other things God says are painful to face up to. If it were up to me, I'd ignore it and leave it quite alone like I've done all of my life up until now."

At the end of our visit I snapped off the tape recorder, thanked Millie, and drove home. Once home I flopped down in the wicker chair in my bedroom, complaining, "O.K. God, what's the deal? I've been a Christian for nearly fifteen years now. So why are you talking so unmistakably and specifically to this newcomer Millie like this and not to me?"

The oddest thing happened. One crystal-clear sentence answered me. The sentence was not spoken, but formed with such split-second clarity that it seemed to come from somewhere beyond my own consciousness. The replying words were, "I have always spoken to you." I gripped the chair arms in shock. I wanted to ask more: how, why, when? But that was all the inner voice said.

I suppose this might be the story of us all. We are so focused on the things we do not know—especially when and if our Wait will end—that we overlook other ways and means in which God speaks to us daily concerning the practical matters we presently are tending. Compounding this problem is the fact that the way God speaks to everyone else always looks so much more dramatic than the way he quietly directs us.

Many books have been written on searching out God's direction. They capably list Scripture references, reason, counsel of fellow Christians, Christian tradition, closed doors, opened doors, the peace of God, conscience, common sense, and prayer. All of these are excellent sources of help. What unites all of these in our inner understanding is the voice of the Holy Spirit, the very one waiting on the other side of the door in Luke 11:13. Jesus says that since the Holy Spirit resides in every Christian, "the Counselor, the Holy Spirit, whom the Father will send in my name, will teach you of everything I have said to you" (John 14:26).

Different people, of course, describe the Holy Spirit's speaking within them in quite different ways. I call it the inner voice. *Voice* is not quite the right word, though, because what comes to me is more akin to a compelling thought. *Inner* fails to describe it entirely, because sometimes the message comes from an outside source. I often wrestle over a problem by writing in my journal, and the answer comes through the ordinary medium of pen and paper. At other times, guidance comes form an unlikely source, just as it did the day I was worrying over a writing rejection, missed a turn, and was forced to make a U-turn on a commercial alleyway that I had never before traversed. I looked up, and there was a green street sign: Trust Street. The street was named after a bank, of course, but God seemed to be telling me that although it felt like I was going backward in my career, I should trust him fully with the matter.

For lack of a better term, we shall continue to refer to our spiritual ability to hear as the inner voice, accepting the fact that this faculty is somehow God speaking to us through a variety of sources and means which we slowly learn to recognize as him.

The inner voice was put to the test over a thorny problem of the Wait with Cindy, a friend of mine. Cindy's son was deeply troubled by mental problems, which caused her to keep asking God over and over, "Will my son ever be well? How long are we going to have to keep dealing with this?" Finally, I told Cindy, "Come over to my house. We're going to sit down and pray about this thing until we get a definite word from God one way or the other."

When Cindy arrived, I stuck a pad of paper and a pencil in her hand, saying, "Write down everything that comes to your mind." We began our prayer time. I started out by quite sweetly asking God Cindy's question. Then I squeezed my eyes shut and waited. And waited. And waited. Finally, I peeked over at the pad of paper. The only marks on it were wrinkly damp spots where Cindy's agonized tears had fallen kersplat, kersplat. I began to get nervous.

After a few more hand-wrenching moments, I heard the pencil scratch out a few words. My relief was short-lived as the sound stopped abruptly. More silence. More tears. I coughed, "Amen." I peered into Cindy's still troubled face. "What have you written?" I croaked, fearing that God had told her something dreadful.

Cindy thrust the pad into my hand, saying dolefully, "It's the same old thing I hear over and over, and it's driving me crazy."

I looked down at the paper. Only two words were written there: "Trust God."

I stared at the paper. In light of our discussion on the inner voice, we must conclude that although Cindy did not understand, God had indeed answered. His word came as a persistent thought that had not gone away over time. The problem was, the reply did not meet her cultural, logical, AB = BA expectations. She had asked an occasion-duration question, and she just knew that the heavenly computer had hit a terrible glitch when she kept receiving a relationship answer. Interestingly enough, the fault did not lie in the answer, but in Cindy's receptivity to it.

Although we may ask God when and if our dreams might come true, our present answer may instead involve knowing with whom the intervening time will be traversed. God's reply is about relationship, presence, and sustenance, not about deadlines and due dates. The Bible overflows with such reassurances of God's nearness no matter what the day, year, or situation. Isaiah says, "Fear not; for I am with thee: be not dismayed; for I am thy God: I will strengthen thee;

yea, I will help thee; yea, I will uphold thee with the right hand of my righteousness" (Isa. 41:10 KJV).

I suppose the disciples might have felt quite like Cindy on the very brink of the ascension when they were still asking (Acts 1:6), "Lord, will you at this time give the Kingdom back to Israel?" I can imagine the disciples being disappointed by the seemingly evasive answer: "It is not for you to know the times or dates the Father has set by his own authority" (Acts 1:7).

The Bible does not identify the questioner, so we shall pick Bartholomew, since he gets little press in the Gospels. Bartholomew is confused by the blunt reply. His logical mind is stewing. *How are we supposed to continue on without even knowing how long we're continuing on or what we're waiting for?* he thinks.

We would like to step into the Scriptures, to nudge Bartholomew, and whisper, "Shh. Listen to what else Jesus has to say. Open your ears and you'll hear your answer plainly enough."

Bartholomew twitches. "My answer? Come on, now. He's already told me point blank he's never going to answer."

Christ patiently continues, "But you will receive power when the Holy Spirit comes on you; and you will be my witnesses in Jerusalem, and in all Judea and Samaria, and to the ends of the earth" (Acts 1:8).

Bartholomew blinks in astonishment. Here indeed is an answer, but it is so unexpected that it has nearly dumbfounded the disciple. Christ has done it again, given a much more useful answer than the one sought. To know what to do in the meantime is infinitely more useful than to simply know a sterile, far-off calendar date. Bartholomew suddenly has a clearly defined task, so well drawn out that it makes geographical sense. Bartholomew is in Jerusalem. Good. He is to begin right there telling others about Christ. Then he is to journey out into the surrounding countryside and farther and farther still until he has reached the very ends of the earth or the very end of his life, whichever comes first. No wonder Jesus does not speak in terms of calendar dates. Bartholomew needs no bigger-than-life occasion to aim for. The rest of Bartholomew's life *is* the occasion and the duration. This *is* the kingdom, beginning now.

In the same way, God has specific "in the meantime" instructions for us all. Of course they include the general, overall picture of discipleship and Christian conduct spelled out plainly in the Bible. On the other hand, other instructions deal with specific personal tasks. These instructions tell us to carefully choose the best thing to do today as we slowly build toward as-of-yet unborn tomorrows.

Such leadings do not need to be as grandiose as preaching in Jerusalem and Samaria. In my life leadings start out small and plain. Taking an adult school class is a common and not very religious thing to do, but for me it was my very first unknowing step toward a writing career. Careful listening is vital, because such guidance is usually in step-by-step, sequential order. The second instruction sometimes doesn't come until after the first step has been taken. That small first step might make sense right away, then again, it might make little sense until much farther along the journey.

This step-by-step pathway is just the thoroughfare we need during the Wait. It is terribly difficult to follow a promise languishing out there somewhere so far away that we can barely see it. It makes sense to simply deal with today's task, believing that in our daily labor, God is leading us closer to our tomorrows.

A Model for Waiting Prayer

One day Joy telephoned me and blurted out, "Pray for my husband." I was quite surprised. We knew each other only casually, and she never had spoken to me about religion. I knew she was desperate when she agreed to let me drop by her house to pray.

When I arrived, Joy had very little else to tell me about her uneasy situation other than to describe her husband as a typical work-focused professional, always poured into his practice, leaving her to deal with all of the childrearing and household work.

Since I was clueless as to where to begin, I decided to try a system I had found useful in the past that seemed to break confusing problems into manageable prayer portions. I asked Joy to get two pieces of paper, one for herself and one for me. On the paper we listed Joy's requests. Let me assure you that this was no child's Christmas wish list; it was a probing and fearless look at Joy's household. The first prayer request Joy put down was that she would discover the root of her husband's despair and hopelessness. For herself, Joy asked for patience, unrelenting support, and love. Joy asked that she might discover what would make her husband feel loved. Joy also requested that their marriage would be made stronger.

We said a short prayer together and then agreed to be in prayer individually and jointly over the list. Our first request was answered with jolting speed. Joy discovered that her husband's crisis of faith was caused by a breech of that faith: he was engaged in an affair with a married woman who sat on a local charitable board with him.

Those who have been utterly betrayed know what Joy went through—anger, insult, sorrow, devastation, feelings of failure, fear. We talked, prayed, cried, and hugged as she poured out her anguish. After the initial shock, Joy decided to weigh her options before she confronted her husband. Prayer became the scales. Prayer also acted as a lid on Joy's anger, a place of refuge, and a place of listening and learning. We prayed for protection for her husband and the other woman, imagining them at the foot of the cross with Christ's blood covering them. During the night as her husband slept, Joy rested her right hand on him, praying silently over and over, "Abba, Father." During other hours, Joy prayed Ephesians 6 for herself, asking God to equip her with the whole armor of God.

After about a month, prayer brought Joy to a place where she finally told God brokenly, "I'm willing to accept my husband and love him as he is, even it if means for now, for whatever reason, he thinks he needs this other woman."

Soon afterward the evening came when Joy was ready to confront her husband. She began, "I know about your affair." Joy's husband replied that he had tried to end things with the other woman three or four times but had failed. His feelings for the woman were immense. He honestly felt he had found the great love of his life, just like the pulp novels pretend. He knew he could lose his family, his practice, and his standing in the entire community over it. He told Joy that he prayed desperately every day, but he felt so alone and despondent that sometimes he felt that the only way out was to end his own life.

During their talk, Joy remained impenetrable to the hurt his words might otherwise have caused. The two talked until nearly three in the morning when Joy whispered, "I think I can help you." She told how God had come into her life in new power when she had admitted her great need for help beyond herself. "We're all sinners," she said, "No one sin is worse. There is an unseen spiritual side to life. You're under attack, and you need the Holy Spirit." Joy put her hands on her husband and prayed boldly for God's forgiveness and for the Holy Spirit to fill him.

We are well enough acquainted with the Wait by now to understand that this was a stunning breakthrough, but it was by no means the end of Joy's difficulties. Although the problem was now out in the open, Joy's husband was unable to make any firm promises. Now came the uneasy period of faith and trust as Joy's husband went about solving the problem in his own way and on his own timetable. His success was quite pitiful at first.

Prayer sustained Joy. We began to see an astonishing link between prayer, guidance, and inner healing. Joy became a truly graceful and grace-full person. The right words and actions presented themselves to her exactly as they were needed, even when just moments before and moments afterward the strength and wisdom were not there. I noted in my journal that Joy became a confident person. There was a clearness in her eyes and a gentle, calm directness of conviction in her voice that had been lacking just a few months earlier.

During this time of uncertainty Joy received two assurances from God through the inner voice. The first was that her husband would return to his faith through her, and the second was that it was God's will that her marriage be healed. The Holy Spirit also told her there were difficulties ahead and that things would get much worse before they got better.

As in all Waits, there were definitely ups and downs. I must confess that a time or two we allowed ourselves to step away from prayer. At those times it was easy to get carried away with suspicions, scheming, judging, and pity parties.

And then there was anger. After things had been dragging along for a year, Joy became worn out with anger. She told God about it, praying for a safe way to ventilate her anger without pouring it all over her husband or her children. Instead of taking away the reason for Joy's anger, God again reshaped Joy's heart. God did not admonish her not to be angry; he simply provided an exercise class where she could sweat off her anger. Then God began to teach her. Joy found something new in John 2:13–17 where Jesus braids a whip to use against the money changers in the temple. This is what Joy wrote about it:

> The anger we feel against the person who is causing our hurt can be divided into two forms of anger: righteous anger and destructive anger. Righteous anger moves us into action. It is a productive anger which seeks God's will. Just as Christ patiently wove the whip of cords, we too can weave a whip of prayer, seeking the authority and will of God to take action.

Destructive anger is paralyzing. It causes us to think only of our will and retribution, our need for justice. It prompts us into reaction, not action. It is the playground for the devil to trip us up, throw sand in our eyes, and tangle us in the web of the self-gratification we feel at hurting those who have hurt us. This anger needs to be cast out of us through prayer and worked out of us physically through rigorous exercise.

During this phase of the Wait, Joy began the slow-going challenge of rebuilding their marriage, sometimes single-handedly. The most astonishing way that the marriage became stronger was that God fashioned a more secure Joy. For many years Joy had felt inferior to her husband because of his boundless business sense, but now Joy had been equalized with heavenly sense. She found herself communicating more openly and effectively with her husband, and in return he seemed more interested in hearing what she had to say.

Despite all of this progress, the day came when things exploded publicly at a charity event when the other woman had imbibed a bit too much Chardonay. The woman put quite a public and aggressive claim on Joy's husband. Afterward Joy and I could do nothing but pray in a heap on the floor in Joy's family room. I cannot remember a thing I prayed, only that I prayed with my arms wrapped around Joy's shoulder as I cradled her head. I somehow wished that my whole body could intercede. I moved through the next hours in burdened prayer, inserting Joy's name as I prayed Psalms 37–44. All the while I was crying out to God, "How could we make so much progress just for this whole thing to end up in shambles?"

After a difficult night, Joy and I met again in the morning to pray. God joined us, even in the muddle. By now Joy was completely used to telling him everything. She surrendered the whole fiasco in prayer and asked God to take over. Then came a moment I find hard to define. In the middle of praying, the expression in Joy's voice changed. To me it sounded like how I might imagine a prophet's voice resonates. It had the ring of the authority of the Holy Spirit on it. The words themselves that Joy was uttering were quite inconsequential. The Presence they invited was not. Suddenly there was nothing else to agonize over, and a strange peace and relief flooded both of us. We parted, feeling that God was indeed, despite it all, in complete control.

Things eventually calmed down, we kept on praying, and Joy kept on rebuilding her marriage. One and one half years after we had begun to pray, Joy glimpsed a farewell letter from the other woman to her husband. Of course, we prayed and rejoiced over it. Her husband was firmly on his journey back toward his heavenly Father; Joy had indeed been the instrument; and their marriage was slowly being reconstructed into something much stronger than the original.

Yes, at the end of the Wait Joy had received the longsought desires of her heart, but during the Wait she had received the greater gift that Luke 11 promises. Joy had received the Holy Spirit. She became filled with power from on high; she became unafraid, strong, gentle, full of faith, and able to face any adversity through prayer. These were the true gifts that last forever.

Conclusion

Communicating with God through prayer is our lifeline during the Wait. Instead of constantly seeking answers, we simply need to seek the constant one who answers. Although we may not receive a sure promise as to what lies ahead at the end of our Wait, we can be given the greater knowledge of God's continual presence and love along the way. Proverbs describes it this way: "Trust in the Lord with all thine heart; and lean not unto thine own understanding. In all thy ways acknowledge him, and he shall direct thy paths" (Prov. 3:5–6 KJV). What leadings have we been overlooking?

Handgrips for Waiting

9

in Pain

That hot August day I did not expect to walk out of the grocery store behind pain and suffering. There I was, jauntily swinging my plastic bag, and there Mrs. Pain and Suffering was in front of me, blocking the automatic door. She was just a stranger to me, an elderly woman of ample frame with a shiny face and neatly cropped hair, moving slowly as she clung to the handle of the grocery cart in front of her.

Her gait was more of a roll, tipping her toward the grocery cart and then around slowly as she pulled each leg forward from the hip without bending the stiffened knee. I glanced down at her legs, sticking out from under her simple cotton shift. I was shocked and repulsed. Her bare legs from knee to ankle were swollen twice the size they should be. They were taut and rubbery and scabbed with dark spots and altogether unhealthy. And there at the bottom of the legs were feet somehow crammed into impossibly little shoes that once fit, shoes that bent and strained at the seams like flattened, leaking vessels.

Even without knowing the woman nor the malady that beset her, everything inside of me screamed for mercy. "Good Lord, surely something more can be done for her! Why on earth is she out shopping on a humid August day? She needs to go home and turn up the air conditioning and prop up those brutalized feet."

None of us expects to meet pain and suffering in the grocery store, and when we do, we engage in the same game of mental volleyball I played. We want a diagnosis as quickly as possible, and then we want the pain fixed, even if it is an ordinary home remedy like foot propping that soothes only the pricked conscious of the outside beholder.

Obviously the woman's problems were deeper and more complex than could be cured immediately, even with modern medicine. And so the woman went to the grocery store suffering, and she drove home suffering, and she arrived home suffering, and she put her groceries into the cupboard while continuing to suffer.

We must begin this chapter with an awful truth. People endure the worst Waits while in pain. Just as we cannot end our Wait, we cannot end or remedy the interim pain and suffering. There are no words we can say that will have any effect on the presence of pain. The pain is terrible, and there is no money or love or kindness or religious formula or surrogate or technological breakthrough or positive way of thinking that will make pain flee from us.

Before we go on, we need to state two basic assumptions about the pain experienced during the Wait. The first, of course, is that it is indeed real, whether it stems from physical or emotional causes. We will part company for a moment and admit that those of us awaiting a positive achievement, such as job advancement or long-sought personal goals, are not suffering to the same degree as others of us for whom the Wait is toward recovery and for whom, in the meantime, there is daily pain. This company might include those awaiting healing from an array of illnesses, accidents, and disabilities as well as those awaiting recovery from emotional devastation such as divorce, bereavement, depression, rejection, and loss. We acknowledge the unmanageable proportions of such pain.

Only the sufferer knows how deeply it hurts, and it does not always necessarily show from the outside with a gaping, bloody wound. In many cases, a sufferer looks normal and is expected to go to work and to pay bills and to take care of the children and to generally smile bravely and get on with the grocery shopping.

Such was Ginny's case. Ginny's husband of fifteen years used the excuse of an insignificant argument to move out of the house. Ginny was shocked, even more so when he refused to come back home and demanded a divorce. The couple had no children, and Ginny had faithfully worked her way through middle age in an office while worrying over the care of her far-away elderly parents. The pain of her mother's lingering death paled in comparison as Ginny now faced her own worst nightmare—the prospect of growing old alone. The only way to adequately describe how Ginny felt is living death.

Ginny could not tell us when she last ate or what she last ate or even anything she wanted to eat presently or ever again. Pain filled her stomach until there was room for nothing else. Sleep escaped Ginny. She paced her bedroom floor all night, crying and rubbing her hands. In exhaustion, she dressed and drove to work in the morning. At work she wept silently at her computer until her head ached, until she could barely read the words swimming on the screen. When she pulled into her driveway at night, a blackness smothered her and she had to force herself to get out and unlock the door. The house was empty, and she was empty and quite broken. The only portion left to her now was the Wait for an end to the pain.

Because pain is so terribly real, we must form our second extremely crucial basic assumption. We cannot leave Ginny sitting alone in her car, the keys trembling in her hand, unable to open her own front door. We shall recognize that a person should endure no pain without seeking all available help. No matter how strong or full of faith we would like to be, there is no substitute for outside professional care. Those in physical pain should be under a doctor's constant and alert treatment. Those in psychological pain should be availing themselves of doctors, psychiatrists, psychologists, counselors, churches, ministries, families, friends, and recovery groups.

Ginny needed intervention. She went to private counseling and received medication that calmed her enough to borrow a few hours sleep. She joined a support group; she talked to friends; she began to make decisions; she went to church and fellowship groups; she formulated her own holiday plans; she made herself eat.

All of these things helped, but none of them put a once-and-for-all end to Ginny's pain. Each was a step in her daily journey toward the end of the Wait when Ginny eventually will be free from pain. Just because she still hurts does not mean that these remedies have failed, it only means that not enough time has yet gone by. Recovery and healing are long-term, slow-going processes.

Outlasting the Pain

Since pain is real and since taking positive steps to deal with it is a long-term endeavor, we are left with only one alternative—to outlast the pain. Therefore, this chapter, of necessity, is not about ending pain but about enduring it. Enduring pain is in itself an act of consummate faith, because such endurance is counter-cultural in a society that would rather stop pain at all costs.

I see enduring our painful Waits as a trip on a subway car. The compartment is crowded; we are forced to stand; the car is rushing pell mell through a dark smothering tunnel; the track is jerky; the car lurches and groans. We go around a curve and suddenly fall sideways. Without thinking we thrust our hand up and grab onto that metal bar bolted to the ceiling.

The handgrip helps stabilize us. The bar does nothing to change the length of the journey nor the track nor the crowded conditions nor our tired legs nor the sudden stops. The bar simply anchors us until we finally reach our station and can gratefully get off. Likewise, this chapter is about handgrips, things that we can hold onto during this painful journey of uncertain length back toward life's daylight.

Paul's Handgrips

The apostle Paul invited himself into this chapter by penning a wonderful God-sized word. My concordance has seventeen references that use this particular word, and I was intrigued to find that ten were written by Paul. What is the word? It's the magnificent King James Version term, *long-suffering*. Webster's dictionary tells us that *long-suffering* means long and patient endurance of offense. To endure means to last, to continue, to remain firm under suffering and misfortune without yielding or giving in.

Long-suffering means much more to Paul than a one-dimensional dictionary definition. To him it is not a simple synonym for *patience*. Paul exhorts us in Colossians 1:11 to be strengthened "with all might according to his glorious power, unto all patience and longsuffering with joyfulness" (KJV). *Long-suffering* is Paul's deliberate word choice in his letter to the Galatians concerning the fruit of the Spirit, "Love, joy, peace, longsuffering, gentleness, goodness, faith" (Gal. 5:22 KJV).

What personal stake does Paul have in this odd, compound word? Historical accounts tell us that Paul, also known by his Hebrew name Saul, was short but solid, bald, bowlegged, and marked with a flushed, hooked nose. Given this nearly comical, Friar Tuck body to live in, Paul sets out early to prove himself a ferocious contender in life by defending with the zealot's fire orthodox Judaism against "infidels," of which the new Christian sect is numbered. He keeps an eye on the cloaks while his compatriots stone Stephen to death. Acts 8:1 says, "And Saul was there, giving approval to his death." The Bible goes on to say that Paul is determined to destroy the entire Christian movement, going from house to house, yanking out men and women, and throwing them into jail.

On one such trip Jesus appears to Paul in a blinding light, and Paul undergoes one of the most radical conversions in history. When we flip the pages forward a number of years, we find this same zealot Paul in Phillippi, so severely beaten as punishment for his now intractable faith in Jesus that Paul bears the scars the rest of his days (see Acts 16:23–34).

After this merciless punishment, Paul is thrown into jail, imprisoned in the same way that he has earlier imprisoned countless other believers in his preconversion days. During the night an earthquake breaks down the stockade door, and the wooden blocks restraining Paul fall undone. Paul defies reason by not only remaining in jail but also by persuading the other prisoners to wait calmly until the jailer brings a torch. This powerful act of will and obedience prevents the suicide of the jailer, the very jailer who has perhaps personally beaten Paul so righteously and severely just hours earlier.

Although the Bible records only the washing of Paul's wounds, we can imagine the anguished scene. A stunned jailer, who should have been dead, helps a wounded Paul, who should have been free. The captor brushes off the rancid jailhouse straw and lice from Paul's outer cloak and with a trembling hand gingerly begins to remove the bloodied shirt. Surely the fabric is stuck with crusted blood. As the jailer carefully peels the shirt from Paul's back, fresh blood mingles with the darkened, dried blood. The jailer takes a clay pot of cool well water and a clean cloth and touches it to the burning, torn skin, trickling water onto every ravaged piece of flesh.

Tears fill the jailer's eyes as the pot of clean water turns red with Paul's mingled blood. He mutters brokenly, "How could I ever have done this to you? What a miserable man I am indeed! What must I do to be saved?"

Tears of past and present pain stain Paul's countenance as he answers back, "Friend, I was a much more miserable man than you! If only Stephen had lived that I might have touched even a drop of cold water on one of the bruises on his holy arms that were held up to heaven. Oh, what a large and long-reaching act of love that I the persecutor was saved! How much more will this same long-suffering Jesus save you and your household!"

In this crucible of personal experience Paul prepares his God-sized concept of long-suffering. Paul writes, "Christ Jesus came into this world to save sinners; of whom I am chief. Howbeit for this cause I obtained mercy, that in me first Jesus Christ might shew forth all long-suffering, for a pattern to them which should hereafter believe on him to life everlasting" (1 Tim. 1:15–16 KJV).

Long-suffering to Paul means God's grace period during which Christ and his people must endure pain, conflict, persecution, and imprisonment—enough time to allow a lost one to be found. Long-suffering is about mercy, love, forgiveness, second chances, and yes, it is about our resolve to live through the pain this might visit on us in the meantime.

God and his people endure Paul's warring madness for the sake of the vast potential for good locked up in his blasphemous soul. Paul is eternally thankful. It allows him to attach the word *joy* to long-suffering; it allows him to take on this grace as a bold way of life. Paul implores us, his fellow believers down through the ages in the Wait, to do likewise.

Long-suffering makes sense in light of the Wait. The pain we might currently experience is not punishment but rather long-suffering. We are now afflicted by others—by wayward husbands and wives, rebellious children, abusive and neglectful parents, hateful neighbors, unkind employers. We are under the thumb of unredeemed institutions: political machines, laws, customs, factions, and profit mongers.

We do not welcome the pain. The pain is not a form of penance for the wrong we have done. Nor will we stay in situations dangerous to our physical or mental well-being or that of our children. Long-suffering does not mean that we will allow the wayward ones to constantly devise scenarios where we are portrayed as the perennial problem. We will not enable their inner sickness, we will not abet their inability and unwillingness to face their own sin. Instead, as the Spirit strengthens, we will endure this time of pain so that others might survive their current rebellion and eventually be saved. Long-suffering is not something we can manufacture. It is the flame of the Holy Spirit kindled within us.

Paul, who was shipwrecked, jailed, flogged, tried, and eventually martyred, writes, "But we have this treasure in jars of clay to show that this all-surpassing power is from God and not from us. We are hard pressed on every side, but not crushed; perplexed, but not in despair; persecuted, but not abandoned; struck down, but not destroyed. We always carry around in our body the death of Jesus, so that the life of Jesus may also be revealed in our body" (2 Cor. 4:7–10).

Paul leaves a legacy for those of us involved in a suffering Wait. We only need open our Bibles to one of his letters and know that the words are addressed quite personally to us. Following is a partial list of Paul's handgrips: Romans 8 and 12; 1 Corinthians 13; 2 Corinthians 4; 2 Corinthians 11:16–12:10; Ephesians 6:10–20; Philippians 4:4–9; Colossians

1:24–29; 1 Thessalonians 5:16–17; 1 Timothy 1:12–17;
2 Timothy 3:10–17.

Everywhere we turn in Paul's writing we find a sure hand-grip fastened to the cross. As we read each letter, we recall the man who knew pain from both sides—as inflicter and as sufferer.

The Lamentations Handgrip

The Book of Lamentations is a five-chapter dirge stuck amidst the fusty, seldom-visited Hebrew prophecies which, having been fulfilled eons ago, have subsequently settled into the dust of history. The very old news of Lamentations is a chronicle of the national disaster that struck Israel in 586 B.C. in accordance with Jeremiah's dire predictions of punishment. Oddly enough, Lamentations still has the power to knock us out of our chairs as we read it, for it records the still-vivid and contemporary news of how suffering makes all time come to a standstill.

In our culture, we think of time only by its precise man-made measurements by the clock. We fail to think beyond to true time—the rhythm that is humming within our bodies such as the cyclical rest, hunger, nourishment, and work patterns. We also tend to ignore the larger seasonal patterns of seedtime and harvest, birth, growth, maturation, old age, and death; we take for granted the societal rhythms of work days, feast days, and holy days.

Because pain does not divorce us from the clock, we often fail to understand how it has disenfranchised us from greater time, which is the ongoing pattern of life unfolding within and without. During our times of pain, we only sense that we are lost in an out-of-sync world gone somehow haywire.

In Lamentations, the clock keeps ticking, but this living-time comes to a halt. There is no longer a harvest; there is no market day; there is no holy day nor Sabbath; there is no daily meal and renourishment; the law is no longer taught; old men do not pass on wisdom; children do not grow but instead die of hunger in their mother's arms.

Today we again enter the Lamentations world when we feel torn from the very fabric of life by long, pain-wracked periods. Night is turned to garish daylight in hospital corridors, mealtimes become lost in knotted stomachs. There is no strength for work, there is no natural sleep. Christmas Day may come on the calendar, but in this setting it seems as artificial as the plastic holly taped to the intensive-care-unit door.

Here in our pain-filled Waits, all past, present, and future time undergoes nuclear meltdown into one hot, vivid prison of the eternal present. At this moment, all living-time is lost, and we feel keenly the cry from Lamentations, "I remember my affliction and my wandering, the bitterness and the gall. I well remember them, and my soul is downcast within me" (Lam. 3:19–20).

We nod grimly in kindred recognition. Then suddenly our fellow sufferer from Lamentations jumps up and peers out of the hospital window, interjecting wild and irrational hope with the next exhalation. "Yet this I call to mind and therefore I have hope" (Lam. 3:21).

We wait breathlessly. What one thing could possibly lift this dark mountain from our breast? Quiet reigns. Our eyes look toward the window. A small drop of reflected grayness dangles against the dark hospital glass. "The Lord's unfailing love," Lamentations whispers. Our head throbs. What unfailing love? Show us a sign that there is still hope, that time goes on.

At the window, the feeble, gray light begins to expand, breathing tentative gray-and-white substance to the whining air conditioning unit on the rooftop below. "And mercy still continue," Lamentations says firmly.

How can mercy continue in this netherworld? The window glows back in reply. The window is now a fading looking glass. The reflection of the sterile hospital room vaporizes as the growing light without transforms the window once again into a portal across the living, breathing world beyond.

"Fresh as the morning," Lamentations says softly. A bird nesting in the emergency room sign makes a soft ta-wheet. Now we understand. Our eyes see the first color emerging from the chaos. It is a delicate pink, threaded just across the angular roof line below. The night is inexorably fleeing. The sun is coming up. The night must flee, for the sun only allows darkness by its absence. The sun has returned to claim the whole land, hospital rooms, lunar rooftops, nesting birds, and fallen Jerusalem.

Lamentations knits all of these thoughts together as a full glorious edge of golden sun turns even the ugly tar and gravel rooftop to pebbles of fire:

> The Lord's unfailing love
> and mercy
> still continue,
> Fresh as the morning,
> as sure as the sunrise.
>
> (Lam. 3:22–23 GNB)

In this Lamentations sunrise we have been transformed into ancient Hebrews, gladly leaving behind our artificial modern-day notion that postmarks at midnight begin a new calendar day. Of course not. We have finished the full course of the night. Now nothing remains for us to traverse but the light-filled day. Finally we understand morning for what it is—God's signature, written across the sky. "The heavens declare the glory of God; the skies proclaim the work of his hands. There is no speech or language where their voice is not heard. Their voice goes out into all the earth, their words to the ends of the world. In the heavens he has pitched a tent for the sun, which is like a bridegroom coming forth . . . like a champion rejoicing to run his course" (Ps. 19:1, 3–5).

We stretch out our hand and clasp the Lamentations handgrip, for it is available for those without a Bible or a church, for those without a preacher, for those hanging onto the slimmest remnants of consciousness. Each dawn is a miniature version of creation as order is renewed out of darkness. We can almost hear the first command, "Let there be light." In the sunrise, despite our pain, we can see ourselves as being created by a master of unspeakable intellect, by one who forms a rebirth from the unconsciousness of sleep into the activity of life.

Lamentations has shown us how simply hope can be reborn. In the Wait, we have been dwelling in an impossible eternity of pain. Part of our anguish has come from projecting our present misery onto every tomorrow. Jesus says, "Do not worry about tomorrow, for tomorrow will worry about itself" (Matt. 6:34). Now we remember. Even during terminal pain there are good days and bad days. We are called upon to live only with today's pain, not tomorrow's. After all, today is so short, so easily finished, and the sun will rise again in the morning; God's promises will be renewed. Although our Wait is not yet finished, we can strangely proclaim with the psalmist, "Weeping may remain for a night, but rejoicing comes in the morning" (Ps. 30:5).

The Abba Handgrip

Someone I trusted and needed had hurt me very deeply. I felt utterly crushed and abandoned. I was driving down the interstate alone. Suddenly my chest sputtered, my face crumpled, and I began to cry. I choked out something I had never said to God before. It came out spontaneously, with no lofty formation nor theological forethought. The words bypassed all pretense, all personal pride. Out of that broken moment I called the Lord of all of the universe Daddy.

It was one of those fragile moments when you realize that some inner barrier has been forever broken. My sorrowful situation had not changed, but great comfort seemed to pour into the car. Daddy God was somehow there.

In the KJV, the word *abba* is used in this same intimate way. Jesus, who taught his disciples to address God with the seemingly lofty and formal "Our Father who art in heaven," prayed under the blood-sweating anguish of his soul in Gethsemane, "Abba, Father, everything is possible for you. Take this cup from me. Yet not what I will, but what you will" (Mark 14:36).

Our friend Paul is again the one who fastens himself to this Abba handgrip, shedding a glorious light on it by explaining, "For you did not receive a spirit that makes you a slave again to fear, but you received the Spirit of sonship. And by him we cry, Abba, Father. The Spirit himself testifies with our spirit that we are God's children" (Rom. 8:15–16).

In Galatians 4:6, Paul once again mentions calling God "Abba," and this time as well it is not a polite, social appellation. Each time we are pictured as crying it out. We are not only helpless, scared children, but we are orphans needing adoption, heavily burdened until we can at last call God Daddy.

I once had a strange dream during a time when I was quite downhearted and oppressed about some serious quarrels at church. In the dream I was in church, singing a hymn. At the end of the song, I closed the hymnal and bent myself into the seat without glancing back behind me. Imagine my shock when I felt myself sit right into someone's lap! As an adult, we are rarely called on to sit in someone's lap, only perhaps when a car is overloaded. If we are put into this delicate and embarrassing position, we try our best to brace ourselves so as not to let our full weight bear on our friend.

With my adult embarrassment intact even within this dream, my body tensed to offer nonverbal apologies for having landed in a stranger's lap. The lap was big and surprisingly soft, and whoever it was did not squirm nor complain under my weight. The stranger seemed to have expected it, as if the purpose in slipping in behind me was to hold me. Without turning to look into the face I suddenly knew that the person holding me was Jesus. All at once that lap was a place of great comfort and rest. Abba was there.

In our Waits of greatest pain and sorrow, we are indeed helpless children, even too short to reach the adult-sized handgrip. That is when Abba silently steps onto the subway car behind us. He puts his left hand up onto the bar suspended from the ceiling, then he offers his own nail-scarred right hand to us. As the subway car speeds on, with our hand enfolded in his, we are admittedly still too weak and small to be on the trip, but suddenly we are strangely unafraid.

Conclusion

Pain may become our unwelcome companion during the Wait. Since we cannot banish it, our only option is to outlast it. But we have been given powerful handgrips of faith by those who have gone before us. And best of all, we all have a daddy to help us through. Have we been trying to handle pain alone?

Ninety-One Miles of Mutton

10

and Other Happy Endings

Trisha Gercken, the hopeful mother from chapter 3, had a detailed scenario planned for the day her Wait would end. On the red-letter day when Trisha finally would receive the long-awaited confirmation of a pregnancy, she planned to hang a bouquet of balloons on the garage door to greet her husband, Joe, when he arrived home from work. In eager anticipation of that day, Trisha bought a package of pink and blue balloons and hid them in the kitchen pantry.

Still inspired by vivid daydreams of the future, Trisha sat down at the typewriter and composed a poem. When Joe burst through the kitchen door with that hopeful, questioning gleam in his eyes, she would hand him the light-hearted verse. Trisha would savor the hallelujah look on Joe's face as he read. When Joe got to the end of the verse and learned that they were finally to become parents, the scene would climax in a wonderful embrace and tears of joy.

That is the way Trisha had it envisioned. Now, here is the way it really happened. One morning Trisha rushed from work to the clinic with severe abdominal pain and underwent an ultrasound. The doctor mouthed grimly, "I see a mass on your right ovary. You're in a pregnancy situation, probably a threatened miscarriage."

Trisha forgot completely about the balloons, poem, and other camera angles and furiously dialed Joe at his office, blabbering, "I had an ultrasound and saw a spot, and I'm bleeding, and there wasn't a heartbeat. But, Joe, it's a baby!" We can only guess Joe's gasping response on the other end of the line.

We all have daydreamed about the end of our Waits. Like Trisha, we have even on occasion vividly planned for the announcement well in advance. Daydreaming is natural. Such reveries can be harmless escape valves; they can help us mentally prepare as we work through how we might handle our future. Daydreams are fine—until we start believing them and trusting them.

One unfortunate hitch of the future is that even when we do finally get our heart's desire, it likely will not match the end-all, be-all fairy tale we have built up in our head during the long dark hours of the Wait. We envision only the overwhelming joy, happiness, and relief that will be ours. We see little more. The purpose of this chapter is to understand that there is, indeed, much more. Welcome to the end of the Wait.

Hollywood, Solomon, and Nehemiah

Just as our culture has clouded our vision throughout the Wait, the mass media feeds us a distorted version of what to expect at the very end. Hollywood stirs our emotions with visions of public adulation: vast, cheering crowds, heroes and heroines basking in the limelight, embraces, tears, triumphant music, ticker tape parades, receptions at the White House, and final declarations of love and loyalty.

After dishing up this grandiose fare, Hollywood heaps more self-gratification onto the platter. According to the script, we also shall be able to relish the utter defeat of our adversaries at the precise moment we are being declared the winners.

No wonder our unheralded endurance victories rarely match our expectations. In real life, there is seldom unanimous, public acclaim or cheering crowds. In our complex and uncertain lives, the enemy is sometimes hard to identify, much less sure to get his or her complete due. To free ourselves from this cultural morass, we will pull the plug on Hollywood and tune in to several biblical endings, starting with the biggest lamb roast in history.

King Solomon throws a titanic feast to dedicate the temple. Although the temple was of modest size by our standards, only ninety feet by thirty feet, it was overlaid with exquisite craftsmanship that required seven backbreaking years of construction (see 1 Kings 6:15–38). There seventy thousand men transported materials, and eighty thousand men cut stone, not to mention the 3,600 foremen and countless artisans (2 Chron. 2:18).

Yet, the seven-year construction project is just a small part of the story. To understand the gigantic size of the Wait, we have to back up another lifetime to King David, Solomon's deceased father. David envisions the temple knowing that he will never even see the foundation started. Nevertheless, David pours himself into detailed planning for the temple building, the courtyards, and even the eventual organization of the priests. In addition, David stockpiles materials: 190 tons of gold, 380 tons of silver, 675 tons of bronze, and 3,750 tons of iron (1 Chron. 29:7).

Even David's lifetime fails to cover the vast Wait. Before David we must back up hundreds of years, generation preceding generation, poking through the graves of Saul,

Samuel, Samson, Gideon, and Joshua, all the way back to Moses. We meet Moses in the wilderness gathering gold bracelets extracted from Egyptian bondage to hammer into a pure gold covering for a box of acacia wood forty-five inches long and twenty-seven inches high and wide (Exod. 25:10–11). This box is the covenant box of God's presence that requires a sacred dwelling place hidden from the eyes of sinful man. Moses is able to fashion only a temporary home of fabric and tent poles against the future time when God might dwell among his people in a permanent temple. That time comes only much later.

Solomon is the one fortunate enough to be alive and well generations afterward at the end of the Wait. The Bible records that to dedicate the temple, 22,000 head of cattle and 120,000 sheep are offered (1 Kings 8:63). If we estimate that each lamb is four feet long from nose to tail, that's 480,000 linear feet of sheep. Put those sheep in a line, and the line would stretch almost ninety-one miles! That is quite a lot of mutton, wool, and chamois. The butchering and cooking of all of those animals defies imagination. Every stream must have been red with blood, and the air must have been thick with the aroma of sizzling fat.

After this matter-of-fact statement about such dizzying quantities the Bible says, "On the following day he sent the people away. They blessed the king and then went home, joyful and glad in heart for all the good things the LORD had done for his servant David and his people Israel" (1 Kings 8:66).

This verse explains that the people possess a dimension of happiness that goes beyond their wise King Solomon, the beautiful temple, and even the national lamb roast. The people are thankful not only for the accomplishment, but also for the long, fruitful relationship with God it represents. Such thankfulness endures, even after their stomachs are empty once again and the pristine temple walls have turned sooty from the constant smoke of the daily sacrifices. The true blessing is God's presence, God's love, God's care, and

God's covenant, flowing in a steady stream from generations past toward generations yet to come.

Hollywood's woeful handicap in such matters is that God's persistent presence cannot be captured by the camera lens. The camera must relay life in concrete, visible terms, which reduces joys to things that only can be seen: the trophy, the new baby, the wedding rings, the final score lighted on the scoreboard, the document in the frame, the embrace of reconciliation. On the other hand, our faith transports us beyond the visible to the invisible. Only one word conveys this type of celebration: *rejoicing*. This feeling is too vast to be contained inside a small, finite human being. At such times, the psalmist imagines all of creation bursting forth in praise. "With trumpets and sound of cornets make a joyful noise before the LORD, the King. Let the sea roar, and the fullness thereof; the world and they that dwell therein. Let the floods clap their hands: let the hills be joyful together" (Ps. 98:6–8 KJV).

One night seven years ago, an interesting Scripture reference came to me that taught me something quite startling about our capacity to be transported beyond earthly news. That particular day I had received a favorable reply from a publisher on a book I had been laboring over for two years, and I was lying in bed, daydreaming about the success and happiness that would soon be mine. Out of nowhere the inner voice interrupted me, "Getting a book published is indeed exciting, but rejoice rather that your name is written in the book of life." It seemed a terribly odd message. Not knowing what else to do with it, I took it to mean that the book would be successful. It turned out I was wrong. Several weeks later the book was abruptly rejected and never published.

I finally understood what God had been trying to tell me. The inner voice had brought to mind a timeless scriptural truth useful for both heady achievement and abject failure. The verse that I recalled that night is from Luke 10. The disciples return to Jesus enthusiastically reporting their personal success in casting out demons. While they still feel this masterful power all over them, Christ tries gently to refocus their joy: "In this rejoice not, that the spirits are subject unto you; but rather rejoice, because your names are written in heaven." (Luke 10:20 KJV).

Jesus points out that although opportune, earthly events can be useful tools in furthering the kingdom, our main reason for rejoicing is the fact that there *is* a kingdom and that our names appear on the membership roster in permanent ink. Oddly enough, this relationship with God has been our source of solace during the Wait; here at the end, it will continue to be our final reason for celebration. Any joy based on event fades; joy based on relationship with God never does.

Just as the movie camera is incapable of depicting our unseen God as the true fountainhead of joy, the camera also cannot portray an ending befitting real-life enemies. The problem lies in the cinematic shorthand which requires that all villains be one dimensional and thoroughly rotten. They can never become complex human beings to us, for we must feel neither pity nor regret when they are annihilated or disgraced.

Before we discuss an evenhanded biblical ending for our oppressors, we must pinpoint who our enemies are during the Wait. The first thing we note is that those opposing us are not a solid, Hollywood, charcoal black. To be sure, some of us have been up against truly evil, deranged individuals and systems that have unmistakably trampled on us. However, the most typical enemy foot soldiers are subtly gray-toned characters beyond the reach of civil law. These opponents are constant doom-and-gloom naysayers about us and our faith. Regardless of their gradations in color, Christ uniformly commands supernatural love for all such enemies (Matt. 5:43–48).

On the other hand are part-time enemies, people with whom we are otherwise happily and normally related: family members, friends, co-workers, neighbors, and compatriots. Jesus experiences this type of enmity when his own key disciple, Peter, becomes a temporary foe of the kingdom by rebuking Jesus for his intentions to undergo death in Jerusalem at the hands of the religious elite (Matt. 16:21–23). In the same way, even those whom we naturally, passionately love become, on occasion, hindering influences when they turn our trusting gaze away from God (see Matt. 10:34–39).

Finally, at other times, we ourselves can become our own worst enemy when besetting sins ruin us (Rom. 7:14–25). Just as no villain is charcoal black, neither are we completely lily white. If Hollywood truly wanted to show complete justice served, I suppose we, the heroes and heroines, should also get a healthy dunking in a mud puddle at the end of the movie.

For all of these reasons, we must reject notions of a Hollywood ending of damnation or ruination for our enemies at the hard-fought end of the Wait. The wheat and the tares, the good and the bad, grow intertwined in the same field and even within the same individual's heart until the final harvest (Matt. 13:29–30).

Despite all of this ambivalence and complexity, the Bible does record a fitting earthly fate for our enemies in the Book of Nehemiah. Nehemiah is a Jewish exile who has, indeed, planted apple trees in Babylon as Jeremiah advises. More than a century has passed; the Persian Empire is overlord of the former nation of Babylon; the Jewish exiles have been allowed to re-inhabit Jerusalem. Nehemiah becomes the royal cupbearer to King Artaxerxes I of Susa. In this powerful position, Nehemiah cultivates the trust and esteem of the monarch and an adeptness at politics that leads to royal permission and provisions so Nehemiah can return to Jerusalem to rebuild the ruined city wall.

Nehemiah's intent is not good news to rulers of the nearby territories. Sanballat, the governor of Samaria, and several other territorial leaders do everything possible to keep Jerusalem's wall an ancient pile of war rubble. They engage in psychological warfare—derision, rumor mongering, political intrigue, and threats. They then plot terrorist attacks.

Nehemiah deflects them with stouthearted readiness. Every workman has a sword buckled to his belt; he and his men stay clothed for battle day and night, even when they lie down to sleep (Neh. 4:23).

Finally, "after fifty-two days of work the entire wall was finished on the twenty-fifth day of the month of Elul. When our enemies in the surrounding nations heard this, they realized they had lost face, since everyone knew that the work had been done with God's help" (Neh. 6:15–16 GNB).

Here it is for us, magnificent in its simplicity, the only tidy and just ending for enemies at the end of the Wait while it still is not yet the end of the age. The boasts of the enemies are silenced. We need do nothing but endure and outlast their insults. We need not silence them with guns nor censure. Our life of faithful endings is eloquent testimony enough against the folly of their deceit. The enemies within and without lose face because it is obvious our accomplishments have come through God's sure and mighty help. Nehemiah's wall is finished and so is our Wait. It is an irrefutable fact. The enemies and naysayers have been shown to be dreadfully wrong, and God has been shown to be abundantly right.

The beauty in this ending is that our enemies never even need to know about our triumph, much less acknowledge it as a decisive personal defeat to themselves. It remains completely decisive and real because the acknowledgement instead comes from God, from inside ourselves, and from those around about us who now turn thoughtful eyes of respect and allegiance toward the God of Israel who is a very present help in times of trouble.

Peter on the Doorstep and Other Strange Twists to Our Endings

Here at the end of our Wait, even with these two sure facts firmly in place concerning God's exaltation and the enemy's loss of face, are more surprises. Such a surprise comes to Rhoda. Rhoda is a servant girl who works in the home of Mary, the mother of Mark. James has just been executed, and the household is now in fervent life-and-death prayer over the fate of Peter, who is imprisoned while awaiting trial. Late into the night, Rhoda is roused by a knock on the outer door and is stunned to recognize the voice of Peter. She immediately jumps up to deliver the incomprehensible news to the household. There is only one problem: In her hurry to spread the glad tidings, Rhoda forgets to let Peter in.

The Bible says Peter keeps on knocking. We can nearly hear him: Bam, bam, bam! "Rhoda, where are you? Open up! Every cutthroat that roams Jerusalem is out tonight. I've just escaped from Herod's jail and I'm expecting to smell the sulfurous torches of soldiers any minute. For the love of life, Rhoda, let me in!" (see Acts 12:16).

Finally, the aroused household unbolts the door. Peter hastily explains how an angel has rescued him from jail. Peter goes on to a safer haven that night and then on to a long and productive apostleship; Rhoda goes on to be remembered in the weighty Acts of the Apostles as the girl who, in a moment of forgetful joy, leaves Peter standing at the door.

I imagine that at the end of the Wait, we shall all be like Rhoda. We shall all smile. It partly will be the joyous smile of celebration, a smile big enough for ninety-one miles of mutton, a smile peaceful enough to give God the glory and rob all credence from the counterclaims of the enemy. But it might also be a smile of good-humored recognition. In effect, we will be quite surprised, perhaps not by the coveted event but by ourselves, our outlandish daydreams, and about the strange way celebrations have of catching us breathlessly unawares.

Trisha Gercken got a second chance at creating an unforgettable announcement for her husband, Joe, one May day when her daughter, Erica, was two-and-a-half. That day Trisha learned that she was unexpectedly pregnant a second time without any medical intervention. This time she drove straight to Joe's office and presented herself at Joe's desk with tears streaming down her cheeks. "Joe, I have to speak to you." By now the whole office staff was gawking, and Joe, thinking something was dreadfully wrong, hurried Trisha to a back room where she declared, "Christmas is going to be messed up this year."

"Why? What's wrong?" Joe asked in alarm.

"Because that's when our baby is due."

Joe laughed out loud, and the next thing Trisha knew, he was running all through the office, announcing their unexpected good news.

Like Rhoda and Joe, few of us mind when joy finds us unawares. What we usually do not anticipate is other reactions that might also catch us by surprise when our long-awaited moment comes. The day of days when I received my first acceptance of a book, it came as a matter-of-fact telephone call. I calmly chatted about completion dates for the manuscript. After I hung up the phone, I did not scream or dance. I suppose I was still having trouble believing it. The first thing I did was wander into the kitchen and clear the dirty breakfast dishes from the counter.

I cannot explain why I did it. Perhaps the dishes made the moment both real and balanced. Those breakfast dishes represented utter, practical normalcy in the face of change. Parts of my life were still safely the same; parts of my life would never be the same again.

The same holds for all dreams that come true. For instance, after the first blush of joy wears off, those who have been awaiting a child are now thrust into the round-the-clock care of an infant with an eighteen-year minimum commitment stretching before them. No matter how long-sought the child, there will be moments of drudgery, uncertainty, and fatigue. It even is possible to feel let down and depressed once the initial excitement wears off. There could be a twinge of sorrow about someone dear who is not there to share the joy, or even later, regret over the adult freedom that is left behind for the responsibilities of parenthood.

This same array of mind-boggling adjustments goes into every ended Wait: marriage, remarriage, recovery, achievement, reconciliation, promotion, regained health, a new career. We cannot make any of the transitions beforehand. We are, in effect, stepping out into space.

This uneasiness is normal, and now the same God who has been with us during the Wait has something else to offer us. I discovered this providence one day when I literally panicked after being given the chance of a lifetime. I had just received the monumental good news that the magazine *Guideposts* had decided to name me a contributing editor. As soon as I hung up the phone, my throat tightened. Where was I ever going to come up with enough good story ideas to fulfill this agreement?

My heart pounded as I reviewed the recent stories that had been nearly direct gifts from God, miracles in how they had found me. Take the story I had gotten fifth hand from my sister's friend's brother's preacher who repeated a story about one of his colleague's parishioners? The news had traveled four hundred miles by word of mouth over a month's time. It was a miracle plain and simple that there was even a kernel of truth in the story by the time I got it!

I sat down and scribbled in my journal all of these fears about not being able to supply good stories. I had just finished jotting down how it would take a miracle to replicate this past good fortune when a realization came. I wrote, "How silly of me to be sitting here thinking that all of a sudden, after all of this time, I now must start providing story ideas for myself! If God has indeed miraculously provided the ones in the past, he will certainly continue to do it for me now and in the future. It's the same old trust I've been practicing all along, just under a new set of circumstances."

Here we must stop to rely on God for one final grace of the Wait. We must rely on him as the completer here at the end, just as we have relied on him as the sustainer throughout the entire Wait. Long-suffering Paul says, "Being confident of this, that he who began a good work in you will carry it on to completion until the day of Christ Jesus" (Phil. 1:6).

We, of course, have a significant part to play. Paul also admonishes, "Now finish the work, so that your eager willingness to do it may be matched by your completion of it, according to your means" (2 Cor. 8:11). What means do we now have that we did not have at the beginning of the Wait? We have ramrod faith that has been tempered, tested, stretched, and expanded.

Solomon's temple did not stand indefinitely. There are many reasons. I wonder if some of it had to do with complacency. Perhaps the people viewed the lovely building too much as a magical ending point instead of a challenging starting point. Perhaps the people of the nation felt they had arrived and that their work was finally done. God was in the nice, golden box behind the stone wall, and life would be easy now.

Instead, I believe that Paul might be urging us, "On with it, then! Do not sit back. This is not the end but the glorious beginning we have been working toward since the beginning of the Wait. Employ all of the character, faith, determination, and trust we have developed along the way."

These gifts of the Wait are indeed the abundant harvest, ready to serve us well now. We have so much to offer. We no longer anxiously await our time of opportunity in the world; the world, strangely enough, now anxiously awaits us (Rom. 8:19).

Conclusion

At the end of the Wait we find ourselves paupers no longer, for all along we have been raised as children of the King. The Wait, which intended to rob us, has instead been the proving ground where we finally claim our true riches of faith.

It is true that we have endured hunger and pain. We have learned to refute circumstance by trusting in God's affirmation of who we are in his sight. We have survived rude exile by creating within captivity pleasant abodes set about with fruitful orchards.

We have dealt with our unwelcome companions of the Wait—guilt and envy and fear. In their place we have invited our friend laughter back into our lives. We have learned the straightforward art of communication with God, and have come to a place where we know how to listen.

In all of these things we are completely victorious. We are possessors of an eternal treasure that can never be wrested from us. We have, at long last, defied the slow-going odds of the Wait. We realize suddenly that our wagons are no longer broken down. We now are quite ready to roll on, wherever God leads us.